YOU ONLY FALL IN LOVE THREE TIMES

You Only
Fall in *Love*
Three Times

*The Secret Search
for Our Twin Flame*

KATE ROSE

A TARCHERPERIGEE BOOK

tarcherperigee

An imprint of Penguin Random House LLC
penguinrandomhouse.com

TarcherPerigee with tp colophon is a registered trademark of Penguin Random House LLC.

Most Tarcher/Penguin books are available at special quantity discounts for
bulk purchase for sales promotions, premiums, fund-raising, and educational needs.
Special books or book excerpts also can be created to fit specific needs.
For details, write: SpecialMarkets@penguinrandomhouse.com.

ISBN 9780525542728

Printed in the United States of America
7th Printing

Book design by Kristin del Rosario
Interior art: abstract flames by VikaSuh/Shutterstock.com

This is dedicated to all who have wondered if they should just give up hope of finding their forever love, who have wondered if they are destined to be alone forever—please keep going, keep trusting, and know that love always arrives right on time. This is also for all my own loves: all of those whom I have already experienced and those I have yet to. And to my incredible daughters, Emma and Abigail, who will always be my greatest love story.

Contents

My Dear Sweet Wild Woman,

Perhaps you have asked yourself why you haven't yet found your forever love?

Only when you have learned all you need to about what love *isn't* will you finally be ready to experience what it *is*. Only then will you meet the person who is brave enough to love you just as you are.

Perhaps you will meet this wild-eyed warrior over tumblers of sweet whiskey, or it will be a chance encounter when the local barista mistakes your double tall for his mocha grande. Maybe you have met him before, but time had to move mountains to create this moment when you are finally able to see him for who he really is . . .

Whenever that moment arrives—you will know.

It was never about you being too much woman, my dear, but about you being too much for someone who didn't yet realize that he was enough.

And when you meet this man who is brave enough to love you, my dear sweet wild woman, you will be thankful that it never worked out with anyone else.

Not only that, you will understand how each previous love was a north star directing you into his arms, because the reality for most of us is we simply aren't ready for our first love to be our last. Or our second love either. At the time, each of these loves has seemed heartbreakingly impossible to move on from, but as the days and months pass, we suddenly realize that what we thought was a good fit was only us wishing it so.

You've hit enough walls and felt the cold rush of air from doors being slammed in your face to understand that the only love you deserve is the one who will meet you halfway. Because the only one who is brave enough to love a woman like you is also the only one who deserves your love. You are unique and special in your thunderstorm of contradictions. Don't ever let anyone tell you differently.

There is magic in the way that you take the mundane and transform it into something beautiful.

Your simple smile can make knees weak and hearts tremble. And it's not your fault that every other man before this one was just too caught up in his own storms to really notice you, because the truth is, it was never meant to last before now.

You are a woman who bathes herself in the lemony essence of hope each morning, washing herself of yesterday's mistakes in order to take on the challenges of a new day.

You are a woman who dances in the rain with stardust still sparkling upon your heels from the last time you followed the insanity of your dreams.

You've always known that you were meant for love, and when you stumble upon the man who just can't seem to get enough of you, you'll know that he possesses the courage that every other lover lacked.

Perhaps this man will not appear to be the warrior you seek. Maybe he is tarnished from all the tears he has shed along his own journey, but what he will show you is the bravery of a man who never fears the intensity of your gaze.

He won't be scared off, and he won't let you talk yourself out of love, either, because this man will have spent his life dreaming of a woman exactly like you.

This man, your warrior, your twin flame, will show you not only why he had to be your third love, but why the others had to come before him, and why every tear you've ever shed over love will have served a purpose.

Because occasionally we meet someone who makes us throw out the rule book for love.

You were born different into a world that celebrates similarities, and though it has been hard to honor your uniqueness, when you meet this man, you will finally understand why. It's never been about whether or not you are like everyone else, and it's never been because you aren't worthy of being loved. Because all you ever needed, my sweet wild woman, is simply a man who is brave enough to love a woman like you.

No doubt there have been men you've stumbled onto, wondering if they were the one, or the beds of men you've rolled out of wondering if the sex could get any better. Then there might have been those who made you forget that you ever thought there was more to life than just behaving well so that you could be accepted by others.

Perhaps you have tasted love but, until now, love has never devoured you.

And while you don't have a desire to dissolve into your lover, the truth is that you want to be ravished, you want to feel love in your bones and the ecstasy of freedom blowing through the tendrils of your hair.

The thing is, my dear, you want it all.

You want the love that time lies down for—the one that twirls you around so fast you spin like the stars above. Yet it must go slow like luscious Southern honey, and taste just as sweet. This love needs to be strong, yet soft enough to comfort you on your hardest days. You want to know what's to come, yet there should be moments as unexpected as shooting stars flashing across the darkened night sky.

And who ever told you that you were wrong for wanting it all? Why has this become an unrealistic standard? I suppose the biggest question of all is, why did you believe them?

The reality is that sometimes the path to forever takes longer than we expected.

I wish that I could say there is a formula for love, and if you follow it, you'll end up happy, but you've tried that. Whether he stayed for two years leaving only debt and worn-out sneakers under the bed, or your only memory of love is the children that came from it, whatever happened was worth it because it's brought you to this moment.

You've tried it every which way, and probably then some. You've read all the latest self-help books, purchased the latest shade of lipstick, and that dress that seemed to suit the part, and still you find yourself going to bed alone each evening wondering what you are doing wrong and why it seems that everyone is happy except you.

Well, what if you are doing everything right?

What if you needed to travel this journey that you're on, not because it's hard, but because the most difficult journey any of us will ever take is the journey to our core, to our own true self.

It has hurt and burned holes into your soul leaving you wondering if you'll be alone forever, or if there is a man out there who is wild enough to run with you at midnight chasing away the what-ifs and reimagining a life where we give ourselves permission to live from our hearts.

But the thing is, you can't attract what you want until you let yourself become who you really are.

It's scary to embrace those darkest parts of ourselves, the same parts that we were told to fold and tuck neatly inside because it wasn't polite to let our crazy show. Instead of seeing them as amazing—or as what sets us apart from the Stepford mannequins who say please and thank you but never bleed for what they want—we cover them up; we swallow them down, until we're choking on our own truth.

We essentially bury not only the best parts of ourselves, but also those parts that make up who we truly are because deep down we fear that no one could ever fully accept and love us for just being, well, us.

Until you embrace the fierce wildness flowing through your veins, you'll never be able to recognize the kindred light in the eyes of a man who has been looking for a woman just like you, even if he doesn't know it. You've been ingrained with a desire for more; so has he, and he has been traveling along his path making his way through his first two loves so that he will be ready for you and his forever.

My dear sweet wild woman, are you ready to embrace your wild? Are you ready to open up and believe in forever again despite the heartache and all the logical reasons not to?

Are you prepared to leave behind the woman they told you to be and the life they expected you to live? It's time to forgive our past, make peace with who we were and who we loved, and take off down the road unknown, the one that leads to passion and creativity, spontaneity, and the love we've only yet dreamed of.

What Is the Purpose of Love?

At first, we think that Love is the thing that slays dragons or puts demons to sleep—it's the force that keeps us safe in the strong arms of our lover. As we grow older and have our hearts cracked or even broken a few times, it occurs to us that Love might just be a kind of currency, something to barter and trade, though what we truly want can remain a mystery.

We begin to wonder: Does Love even exist?

The truth is that Love is countless small moments all wrapped up in the never-ending action of choosing to show someone—over and over again—that we care.

Love is a noun *and* a verb. It's the tears that dampen the soft flannel shirt of our lover as we surrender to the chaos of life, and it's the two a.m. laughter in the dark that makes our stomachs hurt while the rest of the world sleeps. Love is both a feeling and an action, a way of expressing the deep emotion in our soul that we have for another.

But Love is so much more. It's the never-ceasing drive to become better and do better—and also to encourage our partner to do the same. Love is the vehicle by which we learn, we grow, and we evolve into a more conscious and beautiful version of ourselves.

In truth, Love is the means by which we learn how to be in relationship with ourselves, others, and the world. We are not born knowing the rules for successful relationships or which tools we need in order to build happiness. Instead, we learn the hard way. Through trial and a whole lotta errors, we not only come to know what love is but also how it feels to most authentically practice it.

We are mistaken when we believe that love is simply a matter of relationship with a partner. There are actually three stages of love we grow through before attaining our best self. Just as we aren't born running, we also rarely are able to love wholeheartedly and forever the first time around. Instead, we are meant to move through trauma, sadness, and the desires of our ego in order to transcend what we thought Love was and discover what it truly is.

Sometimes I wonder if I had met my third love when we were younger, before marriage, before children, if he and I would have been able to bypass all of our lessons and get straight to the happy bit. But in the mirror of self-reflection I realize that for me, and I suspect for all of us, it would have been impossible because I wouldn't have been the me that he needed so he could become his best possible self.

I look back on my loves and not only is each one different, but they each brought out different versions of me, and while it sounds sweet to wish my first love could have been my only love, the reality is that this is rarely the way Love works.

Love comes sweeping in when we least expect it, and not to make our lives easier or to placate our desires; it comes to help us make the journey home to ourselves.

Because Love is the force by which the universe turns; the beat of our hearts, the feel of a soulful kiss, and the fulfillment of the universal desire we all have to be known, to be appreciated, and to be cared for exactly as we are. Love does not concern itself with adornments, only with the real.

Love is the force by which we move, grow, and transcend even our own perceived limitations. Love should make us better.

Love simply is not only all there is—Love is everything.

We Only Fall in Love Three Times
in Our Lifetime

Regardless of who we are or where we live, we all experience only three archetypal kinds of love in our lifetime. More important, two of these loves—the soul mate and the karmic love—share a common purpose: they must ultimately end so that space can be made for our third and final love, our twin flame.

When our soul mate love ends, often we are left wondering if we will ever love again. By the end of our karmic passion, we may be ready to swear off love for good, preferring to keep company with cynicism on those long evenings. So when our third comes knocking, despite however much our heart is thumping around in our chest begging us to give it one more try, our logical mind isn't sure we can take any more.

The truth is that we need to travel through these three loves for the lessons they teach us about who we are and what we truly want.

NO LOVE STORY IS GREAT BECAUSE IT'S EASY

In those moments when my clients are facing a challenge or obstacle in their relationship, I often tell them that no love story is great because it's easy. No romantic blockbuster makes it to the big screen because the happy ending occurs at the beginning of the movie!

So many of us become frustrated when love doesn't happen on our time line or the way we expect it to. We endure those bitter remarks from friends who have our best interests at heart, telling us if he wanted to be with us he would be. That may be true, but in terms of love, there is no one size fits all.

Sometimes he really does want to be with us—but the timing just isn't right.

While it is beneficial for our personal growth to be aware of which love we've experienced or are in, there is also no way to rush through this process in order to arrive at our third love more quickly.

It's important to remember that there are illuminating moments within all our loves, and memories that we will have forever, no matter which direction our hearts move us. Learning about ourselves and life through our three loves is an awesome process, a journey that will take us from abandoning what we're taught about love as children through being brave enough to define love for ourselves.

The journey is as much about what love is as it is about who we are.

OUR SOUL MATE

Soul mate love teaches us what it means to be in connection with another. This is often the first kind of relationship we experience, when we are young, in high school or just after, when we are starry-eyed idealists. Boy meets girl, boy and girl fall in love, and perhaps marry: happily ever after.

This is the fairy tale we read about as children.

Before we can really know ourselves, we follow the instruction of those fairy tales: what we feel we should be doing for society's sake, our families' sake, or even our own personal beliefs based on their instruction. We believe that this will be our only love. It doesn't matter if it doesn't feel quite right, or if we find ourselves having to swallow some personal truths to make it work—after all, what do *we* know? Clearly, this is what love is supposed to be. Because it is based on family or societal norms, this love won't challenge us much; it doesn't create waves.

Often, this love is from the same geographical area and socioeconomic background. They may be literally the person our parents have always envisioned for us. It will be easy; and because of the approval and encouragement we receive, we won't pay attention to why something just feels off inside our heart.

In this type of love, we rely more on how others view us than how we actually feel.

This first love is our soul mate. For me, my soul mate was my high school sweetheart. It was innocent love, sweet love, and I had nothing else to compare it to.

We fall in love easily, perhaps it's even love at first sight. A soul mate, like our soul family, can be the soul we meet many times, lifetime after lifetime, until we become good friends. This person feels comfortable and we mistakenly believe this feeling will last forever. We might become engaged or even marry. Sometimes we leave them and move on for good.

Our soul mate can also return to our lives to help us heal and move from one life phase to another by providing us with a safe landing pad, which we may desperately need after our karmic love. We know what's expected of us in this relationship, and even if it's not everything that deep down we know we want or need, we sometimes hide out here because the thought of moving ahead into the unknown becomes too terrifying.

And whether this relationship is right or feels right, the most important aspect of this love is that, from the outside anyway, it simply just looks right.

OUR KARMIC LOVE

This is the hard love, the one that teaches us lessons about who we are, and how we want and need to be loved. This is the kind of love that often hurts, through the tough lessons of lies, pain, or manipulation.

We have both wants and needs, and when we begin to enter relationships, we're not aware of the difference or even importance of having both. Our wants are negotiable, but our core needs are not (more on that later). This is one lesson that the karmic relationship teaches.

This love often sneaks up on us because it's not going to be anything like our soul mate. It's going to be shocking, even electric. Instead of a slow and steady burn, it will start off fast and hot. Because we are too caught up in the cycle of arguments followed by passionate making up, we don't realize how deeply we're already hurting.

The hardest aspect of this relationship is that we just don't understand why we can't get it right. It seems only a fraction away from our ideal love! We still think that we will make ourselves worthy of love by somehow behaving in ways that please our partner. But each time we try to make it right, it ends worse than before.

In my second love, I wore my rose-colored glasses for far too long. I had wanted the story line so much that I ignored the reality, and so I was willing to stay silent. It was easier to stay and deal with the devil I knew than take a risk and see what true happiness felt like. At this stage of love, we are still looking for happiness outside of ourselves; we assume the relationship is the problem and we can fix it, rather than realizing that the unhappiness comes from our unhappiness with ourselves and our choices.

In both first and second loves, fear comes into play: fear of what other people will think or say, of losing our partner's love, fear about how to make it work, how to know when to end it, how to know when (and how) to move on. We haven't yet come home to ourselves and so we keep looking for answers outside ourselves.

Sometimes our second love is unhealthy, unbalanced, or narcissistic. There may be emotional and/or mental manipulation or abuse, even physical abuse. Most likely there will be high levels of drama. This is exactly what keeps us addicted to this story line: the emotional roller coaster of extreme highs and lows. Like a junkie trying to get a fix, we hold on tight through the lows waiting for the highs.

The bad news is, our second love can become a cycle, often one we keep repeating with different partners because we think that somehow the ending will be different.

The good news is that this hard love comes to us so that we can work through all our ugly shit and move forward. Through this love, we will become the people we never thought possible; we'll do things that we never could have imagined. It's the love that we wished was right, even though it never will be.

This love is going to challenge us, not only in terms of what we are willing to do for love, but also who we're willing to hurt in the process. For most of us, it will be ourselves.

Trying to make the relationship work becomes more important than whether it should. Never do we stop to consider if we should even be doing all this work. We invest our worth in the relationship's success, so it ends by destroying our sense of self. But this is only the beginning. For now we can begin to rebuild, to finally embark on our path of self-discovery.

OUR TWIN FLAME

This is the love we never see coming. We are finally whole now and on our own, and this person complements us in unforeseen ways—and also challenges us in the best ways possible. These types of loves are not always easy, because the purpose of our third love isn't just to be in relationship with each other but also to grow as individuals into our best possible selves. This is the one who usually looks all wrong for us, or at least that's what we first believe when we meet them. They seem to destroy any lingering ideals we cling to about what love is supposed to be. But in the final analysis, this love comes so easily it doesn't seem possible; the connection can't be explained and knocks us off our feet.

By now either we have sworn off love or run back to the safety of our soul mates. Especially after the disaster of our second love, it's difficult to trust that this time around it could actually be different. By now we are usually older, with either significant relationships or previous marriages under our belts. We may have children. It can just seem easier to stay clear of love altogether rather than risk heartbreak again.

But no matter how hard or how long we resist this love, eventually we realize that it wormed its way in when we weren't looking. Suddenly the very thing we had gone to great lengths to avoid has manifested itself and we are in love again, for the third and final time.

This is the love where we come together with someone and it just fits—there aren't any ideals or expectations about how each person should be acting, nor is there pressure to become someone else. We are simply accepted for who we already are—and it shakes us to our core. At this point we only have struggled in love, trying either to have it fulfill us or to make it work, so just the sheer effortlessness that permeates this relationship is unnerving. The struggle now is to grasp that there can be love without having to fight for it, and that love can in fact come gently without even being asked to.

It isn't what we envisioned love would look like, nor does it abide by the old rules that we followed, hoping to play it safe; it shatters all our preconceived notions. This love often will not only go against all we had thought would be true about our forever partner, but also against old expectations of what a relationship is supposed to encompass.

We may learn lessons from our first two loves, but only in the third are we asked to walk our talk. Not just to be aware of what we've learned or who we've become, but to actually make different choices. Our third love is the chance to do it right because we're finally in the place to know that difference.

This is the love that keeps knocking on our door regardless of how long it takes us to answer, because when someone is our forever, there's no way to ruin it. It's the love we can't run away from.

Because no matter how impossible it may seem, or how unlikely the package it comes in, it's the love that just feels right.

We may not all experience all three kinds of love in this lifetime, but perhaps that's just because we aren't ready. If we are still trapped in the cycles of our first and second loves, there is no way we will be ready to welcome the third.

We may need a whole lifetime to learn each lesson, or maybe, if we're lucky, it will only take a few years.

THE LUCKY ONES

And then there are the people who fall in love once and find it lasts, passionately, until their final breath. Those faded and worn pictures of our grandparents who seem just as in love at age eighty as they did in their wedding picture. These rare gems aren't meant to travel through the three lessons in love that the rest of us are, but it still leaves us wondering if we really know how to love at all.

Yet it's not that these couples were so much lucky as they were able to grow and develop together. These individuals were able to learn the same lessons as those who go through their actual three loves—their purpose was just to do it side by side in this life. Neither way is more right or wrong, or more difficult, but merely what our souls signed up for prior to this lifetime.

Someone once told me these folks are the lucky ones, and perhaps they are, but I think those of us who make it to our third love are just as lucky, those of us who have given up on love completely from too many nights of sleeping alone.

Because it isn't about whether or not we are ready for love, but rather whether love is ready for us.

What we all must remember is that just because it has never worked out before doesn't mean that it won't work out now.

What it really comes down to is whether we are limited by how we love, or instead if we love without limits. We can all choose to stay with our first love, the one that looks good and will make everyone else happy. We can choose to stay with our second believing that if we don't have to fight for it, then it's not worth having.

Or we can make the choice to believe in the third love.

The one that feels like home without any rationale; the love that isn't like a storm—but rather the quiet peace of the night after.

And maybe there's something special about our first love, and something heartbreakingly unique about our second . . . but there's also just something amazing about our third.

The one we never see coming.

The one that shows us why it never worked out before.

The one that lasts.

And it's that possibility that makes trying again always worthwhile, because the truth is, you never know when you'll stumble into love.

The First *Love,* Our Soul Mate

THE ONE THAT LOOKS RIGHT

PART I

THE DREAM

We'll Live Happily Ever After

When we meet our soul mate love, it seems like it will last forever, whether it occurs at age sixteen or forty-six; one taste of the sweetness of calls that linger late into night, our laughter creating silhouettes around the moon, and we're hooked.

There's no going back in this moment when we first discover love—and we wouldn't even want to because from the first time we encounter this love, we're already writing the story in our heads. We're already signing on to living our lives with this person, savoring thoughts of all that is to come. The feeling of first love is so strong we almost have to believe we have found our forever person.

But the thing is, our first love isn't necessarily our resting place. Often, in hindsight, we realize that this was the person who seemed to "fit" into our life; the one who, more often than not, we've been conditioned by family or society to expect that we'd be with. While we would like to say that the cliché terms of daddy or mommy issues are nothing more than an excuse for bad relationships, the truth is that everything we go through as children shapes our definition not only of what love is, but also what kind of relationship we expect to be in.

It's been decades since my first love, and I can still remember the giddiness that ensued when he would call and how I would lie on my bed with my feet against the wall as I stared out the window thinking that this was the love I was meant for. That somehow, even at the tender age I was, I had discovered within my own life what I had seen play out in the countless movies I'd cried over as an overly romantic and rebellious teenager.

This man—or really boy—fit so many boxes that I needed to check off at the time: He was from a similar background. He was someone with whom I had mutual friends. And being with him seemed so damn easy! Looking back, I can see that it was impossible to not love him because everything came so naturally. But it's only with time and experience that we realize similarities don't necessarily serve as a basis for long-lasting love or even personal satisfaction.

IT JUST FEELS SO COMFORTABLE

With our soul mate, it's often the ease of the relationship that creates a feeling of destiny or even completeness. Our soul mate love is someone that we've traveled through multiple lifetimes with, but unlike the karmic love or twin flame, there are no major lessons to learn from them specifically and there is not the sharing of those mesmerizing energy ties, the strong feelings of connection. It's more like coming home to an old friend, lifetime and lifetime again, so when we stumble across them, it's that feeling of "Oh, there you are, I've been looking for you."

Not because they are everything we want or need but because they are so familiar, so comforting; and that's why some of us have difficulty moving on from this love.

This type of love is perfectly depicted in the movie *Love and Basketball*. The film stars Sanaa Lathan and Omar Epps as Monica and Quincy, next-door neighbors and, ultimately, childhood sweethearts, who share a deep love of basketball. The couple parts ways as college approaches, and the distance between them carries not just the pain of separation, but also the stress of maintaining their respective academic and athletic careers. Their eventual breakup is disheartening, as the two realize that their relationship was based on comfort. Later, they end up getting back together as adults in one of the greatest scenes in the film. Monica and Quincy play one-on-one basketball and reaffirm the essence of soul mate love and what it teaches us.

In order to understand this kind of love, we need to understand that there is more to life than simply this lifetime. Each of us is not just a body, but a soul, a spirit that lives on through multiple lifetimes. Because of this, we each have a soul family, souls that are reincarnated in different forms but that travel through lifetimes together. Sometimes we are friends and lovers, sometimes mother and child, but we stay together. Soul mates are just that—someone who is part of our soul family. This is the reason why soul mates tend to be so difficult to move on from—the comfort level is so high.

Unfortunately, though, we can't continue to grow as souls if we stay where we are only comfortable.

That's not to say that love should be hard, but in order to continue to grow as individuals into our best possible selves, we do need to be challenged, to expand beyond the previous parameters we existed in. And while our soul mates are wonderful and loving, they do not in fact challenge us beyond our comfort zone.

Our soul mate is someone we can return to time and time again only to always have it feel the same.

When considering the complexities of first love, I think of the '90s show *Dawson's Creek*, in which Katie Holmes plays a sweet but complex girl, Joey, from the wrong side of town who falls in love with her childhood friend, Dawson, played by James Van Der Beek. During the course of the many seasons of this show, Joey and Dawson have an on-again, off-again romance in which they fluctuate from being in love to just being friends—that dynamic itself is very indicative of a soul mate relationship.

We never really want to be without our soul mate, and in fact often can't imagine our life without them. In some ways we can even feel lost in the beginning if we separate or begin to move in different directions, which is why sometimes it's often our soul mate who comes back to us during difficult periods of our lives and why we try again with them.

As soul mates tend to meet in their earlier years of life—think childhood, high school, or even those elusive college years in which we drift around sampling relationships—this is often a relationship that we return to later in our lives, if only for a short period of time.

Many times our soul mate can even feel like a fallback solution because they are always there. Sometimes we even marry them (again!) because we start to believe the reason we always go back to them is that we're *meant* to be together.

Even Joey reached a point where she moved on from Dawson and found lasting happiness, but it wasn't until she began to think more about herself and what she wanted that she was able to do so. Part of the problem is often that the fairy tale is just so damn alluring.

We all want to fall in love and have it last—after all, many of us struggle with understanding what the point of love is if it's not going to do just that.

So our first love comes walking into our life and somehow it seems that it's just meant to be. It seems like this person was orchestrated by the hand of fate to be with us, and so we jump all in. Because this relationship often occurs in our younger years, going all in doesn't always mean marriage but it does mean fully committing to the relationship and even dreaming about the future together. It means thinking that forever is a possibility and it means giving in to the part of ourselves that also hopes this isn't only our first love but also our last.

WE ALL WANT A BEAUTIFUL LOVE STORY

We want to run into someone and have it be love at first sight. We want to marry our high school sweetheart. We want the kind of love that we see on the silver screen. The story that we hope to actually live someday because it's not just about the fairy tale but also about life going the way we had planned it would.

One of my clients, Britt, first came to me with her partner at the time. They both believed that the other was their twin flame and they had reached out to me to learn more. After the initial call, she messaged me privately and asked if I could take just her on, independent of her partner, because of feelings of doubt and concern that she was having. This man quite literally treated her like a princess and it felt like a fairy tale. But the thing that we often forget is that fairy tales, even in children's storybooks, have a darkness present in them as well. Over the course of several months that Britt and I worked together, she became strong enough to say that the relationship wasn't what she ultimately wanted and that—even more—it didn't feel good to her soul anymore.

She wasn't able to be who she truly was, she didn't feel completely supported in her journey—but she loved the fairy tale that she and this man had.

Of course there was a period of time where our calls were about processing and her swearing off love indefinitely, saying, "I don't need anyone, for the first time I'm happy as I am." What she didn't know was: that is one of the hallmarks of actually being in the place for that beautiful love story to happen because love usually finds us once we stop looking for it.

Fast-forward a few months after her breakthrough, and she's met her third love. He swept in with such ease, not because they won't have obstacles to work through, but because they are both committed to doing better this time around.

What we think of as a beautiful love story often differs from the way that it actually plays out. We don't get the fairy tale, but we can conquer the darkness. We still can have that love that lasts forever, it's just not likely it will look anything like we thought it would.

This ideal doesn't even start with us. After all, we're still sold on the traditional life plan of graduating from high school, going to college or getting a job, finding someone to marry, settling down, buying a house, and having babies. End of story. That's what everyone does, right? The only problem is that our version of what happily-ever-after is can never be based on other people's beliefs or conceptions.

We need to write our own stories.

Of course, when we are in the thick of our soul mate love, we want to believe we know it all. But it's only with time that we realize how little we actually knew during those early years of our lives, how much we were still learning. In our soul mate relationship, our idea of love is so often based on the person that we are expected to love and, of course, the life we have been told we should live.

As children we are subconsciously taught what romantic love is, through fairy tales, movies, and the stories our own friends and family tell us. It's taught to us in the relationships that we see around us. Rarely do we, as children, sit down with our parents and discuss what the building blocks of a strong relationship are or how vital it is to cultivate self-love. Instead, we hear only the expectation that we find a good man or woman and settle down. That's it. So our soul mate is just that, a good man or woman who seems like someone we should pair up and do life with.

It's a sweet love, perhaps not one that sweeps us off our feet but one that satisfies us to a degree. It is still, though, usually based on the ego. The ego satisfaction that we receive from this love comes from the gratification we gain from the outside world because we're doing what others expect of us. When we are in the early stages of this love, it seems like we are on top of the world and have life figured out. We know our place within our families and even society as a whole; we can see our future clearly laid out in front of us and we breathe easy because, well, everything just seems so comfortable at this point.

Our parents and families love this person, and of course it's no surprise because it's the person they conditioned us to bring home. Our soul mates fit into our family effortlessly, as if they had always been there, in fact, and even more, they tend to feel like family. While we are attracted to our soul mate, the love that we experience with them is more familial, which is part of the enchantment of this connection. We try to have the relationship our family expects us to have, which means during this love we are most often operating under the "I should" rather than the "I want" motivating factor.

This isn't to say that we don't want to build a life with our soul mate; but if we make the choice to go deeper, we will see that it's not necessarily because of a strong love or even connection that we are with them, but rather because they seem like the person others think we fit well with. During this phase of our life, what is most important to us is the approval and opinions of others because it encourages the still developing ego. We haven't yet had the time or experiences in life to discover who we truly are.

PLAYING THE PART

We don't yet know that we can receive the same gratification from making our own choices that we do from simply following along with those we've been conditioned to make.

In fact, during this love, we don't usually question who we are; it's not something that is even on our radar because we think we've got it all figured out. We feel we're growing up in accordance with everyone else in our social circles, doing the same things, making similar choices. Our parents like the person we're dating, so really it seems there isn't more than this.

We don't yet understand that the man or woman we've fallen in love with is little more than a reflection of the person our families have taught us to search for.

Often, while our soul mate is an important person on our journey, they are quite similar to those we were raised by, whether Mom, Dad, or extended family members. Our soul mate is often the person that we see as possessing all the positive qualities of our parents, and it's the origin of the old saying that we marry a man like our father or a woman like our mother. This is our first love, and it's the only one we yet know, and so we honestly fall in love with the person who is similar in nature to our first primary relationships: our caregivers, whether that be parents or someone else who raised us. The pattern of searching for their qualities within our first love is always present regardless of the biology associated with it. It's what we know and so it's what we continue. It gives us an immense amount of gratification because only our soul mate love feels like we're following the rules that we've been given for love and life.

This perhaps is one of the primary reasons why it can be difficult to separate from our soul mate: once we understand that there are no real rules for love, we begin questioning what we *do* know. So often in the beginning we talk ourselves into the happily-ever-after; we talk ourselves into all the reasons to stay, to not deviate from the plan, and ultimately to stay on course with the vision that we have for our life.

However, this really is the vision that we've been taught we should have for our life—not necessarily the one that is authentic for us.

FALLING FOR THE FAIRY TALE

During the early years of my life, I can't say that I thought much beyond marriage, and I see this with countless women that I coach as well. We fall in love expecting the fairy tale even though none of us ever stopped to ask if Cinderella was happy after she said "I do."

I didn't ask myself if my first love would support my growth, if he'd make a good father; I didn't wonder how we'd work through life's issues together or what his spiritual beliefs were. Instead, I saw him just as he presented—his physical self. It wasn't that I ignored anything beyond that; it just wasn't part of my level of awareness at the time because it wasn't how I thought about myself and my own life.

During this fairy-tale stage of love, we aren't sitting around

wondering if we're living our best lives and we certainly aren't thinking about our life's purpose. Even in so many of the movies we've
enjoyed watching, take *Good Deeds*, for example, we didn't hear
about shared goals or purpose as part of their love. No, it was the
"prince"—the man rescuing the damsel in distress and upholding the
traditional gender roles—that we were raised to believe in and to
expect in our own lives.

It was the belief that love was all we really needed and that being
in a relationship with another was what we should aspire to.

Rachel, for example, thought she had her happily-ever-after. She
met this man while going to college overseas, and he seemed like
everything she had ever wanted for her life partner. After graduating, they got married and had a child, life seemed good—until it
became impossible to ignore that it wasn't. In Rachel's case, she got
so caught up in the idea of getting married, having a house and
babies, that she completely overlooked who her husband really was
and the unhealthy behavior that had been present for a long time.

So in Rachel's case, she did get her fairy tale, her happily-ever-
after—it just didn't last as long as she thought it would.

Happily-ever-after, though, is really the belief that from a certain
point on there are no surprises, no deviating from the plan, no dis-
appointments, and certainly no heartbreak. While we can read that
and agree it lacks believability because we all know that there isn't
anything any of us can do to prevent life from happening, the truth
is that living happily ever after isn't the highest form of love that we
can experience. Having everything feel perfect and never going
wrong isn't really what we're hoping for, but rather it's the person

who grabs our hand when we are in darkness and helps us see the light; the person who is there to help care for us when we're sick and have been wearing the same sweatpants for days.

What we truly want from love is not necessarily the person with whom we can have a fairy-tale love, but rather the person who brings magic into the everyday and real-life struggles that we all face.

THE RETURN OF THE SOUL MATE

In hindsight, it may be easy to say all of that once we've been through our first love. But to be enmeshed in the situation and rec-ognize that it's not supposed to last forever is quite another, and this is why, after other heartbreaks, we often return to our soul mate. I remember at one point in my own life after a long and arduous re-lationship finally ended, my soul mate came back into my life (thank you, social media) and it felt like coming home. It didn't matter that it had been thirteen years since we last spoke, we picked up right where we left off with the same comfort and conversation that we had had years ago.

I would never really have sought him out again but that didn't mean he didn't cross my mind; even now he occasionally does. But I also know that with our soul mate, this is expected to be the case—we could meet fifty years from now in a retirement home and still have that instant chemistry and feeling of comfort.

He came at a point in my life when I was truthfully broken, and perhaps the worst part was that I didn't know who I was anymore.

After a few weeks of texting, he asked me to meet for drinks. I wasn't sure what to expect but it felt good, and I knew that regardless of what happened, I was safe with him. Besides, at the time, that was the kind of experience I needed. We met in a cellar bar with just enough dim lighting that it felt like maybe he wouldn't actually see what a mess I was. As I sipped my elderberry martini, as any good hipster in training would, I once again felt like maybe this was it; maybe this man was supposed to be my future. But the truth was in what he did next. As he got ready to excuse himself to use the bathroom, he handed me a note creased with years of being folded and unfolded and said, "Here, I brought this for you, maybe you just need to remember who you are."

I smiled and took it, the candle on our table casting a soft glow on the faded blue ink. Slowly I realized it was a note I had written him over fifteen years ago in which I described the person that I was at the time. I spoke of who I was and what I wanted, what I deserved from love and how I knew he'd regret losing me one day. It was exactly what I needed in the moment because I had forgotten who I was; I had forgotten my own worth and somehow along the road of life I had forgotten the fire I had been born with.

In retrospect, this wonderful, safe man came back into my life to help me remember who I was as a young girl, who I knew I was before the world fucked with my head and made me doubt myself. He came back so that I could then begin the journey to find out who I was meant to be, not to be a part of my future. He was a buffer for me as I made the journey from my past into my future. He helped heal the wounds from the relationship I had just left so that I could begin to move forward on my own. Often when we've been hurt very deeply, however, finding a comfort zone can feel so good. So I tried to convince myself—and him—that we were each other's forever.

It wasn't necessarily because we were all wrong for each other that we didn't make it to that point, but rather that he was my first love, my soul mate, and it was his job as such to come back into my life when I was at my lowest to help propel me toward my next chapter.

Many of us just don't want to leave our soul mates for the simple reason that it seems like love couldn't possibly be any better or bigger after them, but we lack the clarity to put into words why we feel like that. We don't understand that we still have fears around knowing who we are or deviating from the plan we expected to live.

We can't put into words yet that we don't know what we really want from life; having too many possibilities scares us because, well, where do we go from here if anything is possible?

So in retrospect we often stay with our soul mates for longer than we should have just because while we may not grow as souls, we are safe within the comfort zone that they provide. They will never encourage us to grow away from them, so we can become stalled within these relationships. We are content at times in our own lives to love blindly; to stay in something just because it looks right even if it doesn't always feel right.

At this stage, we choose to stay within a love because, at the time, how others view us is more important than how we actually feel or think about our own lives.

BUT I DID EVERYTHING I WAS SUPPOSED TO

Our first love is just the beginning of our journey, it's not yet even a conscious choice to make others happy but to simply want to stay within the status quo. In my work with the amazing women in my coaching program, I see many come to me after they've married and had children with their soul mates, and now they don't understand why they don't feel happier.

In one particular case, an insightful and conscious woman named Anna first contacted me because she was in what we in the spiritually evolving world call the "darkness of the soul" phase in which the ground drops away and it seems you have no idea who you are, where you're going, why you're here—and it feels like the world is ending. This is made all the more difficult because, to the outside world, it seems like everything is fine.

In Anna's case, it was her realization that she wasn't as happy as she thought she should be, even though she had made all the right choices for her life. She married a wonderful man out of college, they had extremely successful jobs, bought a house, had children, and yet here she was at the bottom of her soul feeling suffocated by life and not sure where to turn. How many times have I heard clients say, "But I did everything I was supposed to," to which I always respond, "Yes, girl, that was my problem too."

Our soul mates make it so easy to squeak by with a reasonably good life that we often don't even realize it's not what we truly need until much later. Until we've redecorated the kitchen for the umpteenth time, or finally taken that vacation to the place where it seems everyone else is going and still feel restless that we begin to wonder, "Oh my god, is this really my life; is this really what my life will be like from here on out?" The problem is that in all of the fairy tales and movies we take in, the story ends when they get married; the screen goes dark after the big kiss or the "I do."

In the fairy tale, we never find out what happily-ever-after actually looks like after ten years of marriage and two kids.

Perhaps for some of us who marry our first loves, we essentially get lucky because we found someone that we could grow with despite how much life was guaranteed to change. Even for those few couples who fall into that category, however, I doubt many would say their love ended in happily-ever-after. In some cases I've even heard people say, "We survived our marriage." We should never feel like we are "surviving" a relationship. And so for those fortunate few who found their forever love the first time around, it's really about both people fully accepting each other as they are and the selves they are constantly growing into.

We don't see the full truth of this relationship in the beginning with our first love, our soul mate. We don't see that we're choosing someone based on what we were taught and absorbed from our families. We don't understand that we can't possibly choose a partner for life when we don't really know who we are.

And perhaps most of all, we can't commit to living happily ever after with anyone because life isn't a fairy tale, no matter how many of us wish at times it were.

So we focus on the love and try to forget the warning signs. We overlook how sometimes things just don't feel quite right, or the way that we can't quite imagine growing old with them. We don't want to see the cracks in our connection, because to acknowledge them means that we have to do something about them. When we are in the throes of our soul mate love, nothing really exists except the comfort zone that the relationship creates for us.

We overlook how sometimes we don't feel ourselves with them, that we are not understood completely. How sometimes we look at them and already feel like we've grown beyond them but we don't want to lose the love, so we try to close our eyes. We try to ignore the obvious, the way we get a hollow feeling in our stomachs when our mothers tell us we did good. We look away as we see them disregard something we're interested in or when it becomes clear that maybe we aren't so similar to our soul mate after all, or at least not in the ways that truly matter.

But perhaps most of all we start to become aware of ourselves hanging on to this love, not necessarily because of the person but because of the fairy tale that it represents. We want to ignore the subconscious part of ourselves that recognizes that once we loosen our grip and let our soul mates slide from our fingers, then we're going to have to tackle the difficult job of beginning the journey to find out who we really are.

And when that occurs, we will no longer be able to stay in a relationship that doesn't feel right just because it may look good to the rest of the world—because once we actually commit to finding our own truth, it then becomes impossible to not actually begin to live it.

PART II

THE REALITY

Some Things Just Don't Fit,
No Matter How Hard We Try

We all have those moments where we don't just ignore the red flags, we happily wave to them as we pass because we're hell-bent on sticking with the plans we've made. It's not really about being stubborn (although that is a piece of it), but rather that we can't conceive of what to do if we don't have someone to define who we are.

While there are so many positive qualities about our soul mates, it is this love, more than any of the others, we use to identify who we are to the world. It's easy for us to be fooled into thinking we have it all figured out when we use the visions others have for us to shape the dreams for our lives. But there is another piece, and that is, early on in these soul mate relationships we see glimpses of why ultimately things will end up not working out, but we just don't want to actually acknowledge that at the time.

We don't want to think that this isn't going to last forever, and we don't want to cut short the story line that we've built in our heads.

IGNORING THE SIGNS

What it really comes down to is that we not only sold ourselves on this idea of fairy-tale love, but in the process we neglected to actually find out who we are and what we actually need from a relationship.

My soul mate was a wonderful person, but now that I am in a place where I can be honest, I can look back and see why during the second (and even third) time around it was never going to work. At one point he said to me, "If you didn't have kids, we'd be together." At the time, I dismissed it—which is code for consciously choosing to ignore someone who is saying they can't be what we need. I thought that with time he'd change his mind, after all I always looked at my girls and thought they were so amazing, how could anyone not look at them as a bonus of being with me?

But he was being honest at the time, just as he was when he told me he was looking for the fairy tale: he wanted to get married, have kids, get a house. And while I paused and stuttered a response that sounded like the one I was supposed to give, deep down it was then I really began to know that this wasn't where I was supposed to be.

Our vision for love was different, not because we didn't care about each other or even have a connection, but rather because our core needs were different. I needed someone to accept all of me, my wild, spirited daughters included. I was more focused on being free, on doing things differently, on traveling and making a difference in the world than I was on getting married and starting all over again in the traditional fashion.

And the thing is, that's okay, but where we run into the issue with our soul mate is that we want it to fit.

They are a great person, they make us feel like a better person, and so we hold on to them. We try to convince ourselves that maybe we can be the person they need us to be, never fully realizing that we can't fit ourselves into someone else's mold for their life. We can't be the person our lover wants us to be, we can't live a life that's not true for ourselves, and no matter what, we can't make a relationship work that is destined to end. This one idea is, in truth, where so many of us are who are in relationships that don't truly satisfy our needs—not because the love isn't there but because we can't change someone; we can't change what they want from their lives, or what love means to them.

Especially early on in this relationship, however, we aren't even focusing on ourselves, but only on them: How can we give this person enough so they'll want to stay? How can we compromise so that we can have a life with them? And, of course, how can we change so that they want to be with us?

Never once during this process do we stop to consider if this person is actually what we want; never once do we ask ourselves if they are capable of fulfilling *our* core needs. Because as long as the ego is involved, it's going to constantly pass the work off on another person instead of letting us own it for ourselves.

To anyone from the outside, Leah has the perfect life: an attractive husband, sweet children, and a wonderful career, a life that would be envied. But as we seem to learn as we age, appearances are deceiving, especially in terms of relationships. Leah wasn't happy in her marriage but she didn't feel she had a justifiable reason to leave, so it was easier to try to change who she was. She started giving up things that she enjoyed because he didn't approve, and she stopped talking about things that were important to her because he didn't agree.

Yet all of this was done unconsciously. She never woke up and thought, "I'm going to change who I am to try to make my marriage work," but that is still what ended up happening. It's the gradual concessions that we end up making that add up over time, until we're looking in the mirror one morning wondering how the hell did we get here.

One of the important reasons this relationship is our first is because oftentimes as children we're told to not quit, not give up, to stay with something; and in some ways those were the very guiding principles that facilitated marriages staying together in our grandparents' and parents' time.

I remember sitting with my own grandmother in her kitchen one afternoon, sipping whiskey sours as the low sun filtered through her window and talking about love and marriage. I had just recently divorced and of course was feeling like a pretty big failure; after all, I couldn't make something "work" that so many other people were able to do. While we were talking, she told me that people just didn't divorce during her day—but that didn't mean that the relationships were intact or full of love.

She told me one story about a couple she knew that presented to the entire world as being together and in love, all the while he had moved his bed out to the garage. They were married, they were to-gether, but they weren't truly making it work.

So many times in life we become so fixated on having something that we end up sacrificing our own desires and needs to just keep it around. Soul mates are not going to challenge us to become better versions of ourselves in an obvious way: they aren't going to ask us to step away from the status quo or to ultimately make the choice to find ourselves. That is not their purpose in our lives.

Many of us need to experience what we don't want or what doesn't work before we are motivated to actually move forward in our lives and start making different choices. The only question then becomes how long are we going to keep making something work that actually was never supposed to last?

In the beginning of our romantic journey, we substitute the re-lationship that we're in for our own sense of identity. We are "so-and-so's wife, girlfriend," and so on. The relationship becomes who we are and often it can feel pretty good, especially when we have circles of friends because of that relationship, and our family thinks they're amazing. So we're not just us, but we identify as the people we've become because of our relationship.

This is where ego gets involved in why we choose to stay or leave. Ego wants us to be seen in a positive light by others; ego wants us to succeed, not lose. But ego also doesn't want us to be uncomfortable or uncertain. To change our lives or leave a soul mate means that we have to override this very ego that craves the status, security, and confidence this relationship grants us. Otherwise, we're going to have to figure out who we are apart from the identity of being the wife or girlfriend to our soul mate.

DISCOVERING OUR CORE NEEDS

Soul mates are easy in many ways, but the one difficult and ultimately deciding factor is that we can't be with these types of lovers and also be our true selves—yet this is something we only learn with time. We need our soul mates to define us so that we begin to feel trapped enough to then make the scary choice to discover who we truly are.

We need our soul mates to be easy so that we learn we need to be challenged. Ultimately, we need to first follow the rules for love and happiness so that we can then learn that there are no real rules after all.

Everything in love is a building block in becoming our true selves but also helping us to identify what we need from another person. In relationships, each of us has core needs in order to feel happy, in love, and satisfied with our partners and our lives in general. When one of these needs is not being met, we feel confusion because everything else is so good; that is when we try to make it fit even though it's not meant to. This leads to the subconscious decision to try to fit someone into a space that we have in our lives, even though they are unable to fill it as their authentic selves.

Our core needs are not only the motivator for any relationship we enter into, they are also the barometer for whether it will last or not.

Core needs are different for each of us depending on who we are and what phase of life we are in. Even the same person at varying phases will have a different set of core needs. Think back to your twenties, or even teens. What we needed from a partner was likely more socially based. We wanted someone we could have fun with, someone who was convenient, someone we enjoyed kissing and who would also fit in with our friends as well. As we get older, those needs change to someone who would be a good parent, someone who seems like they'd be a good husband or wife, someone who is financially stable.

Yet as long as we're setting our core needs based on external factors, then we will never feel truly fulfilled.

As we transition through relationships, what we need from a partner changes. Instead of looking for someone who seems like they'd fit in with our friends or be a good provider, we begin to crave someone who appeals more to our soul needs. This could mean that a prospective partner's sense of spirituality, consciousness, or awareness becomes important to us because it's now something that we value as a part of ourselves. It's likely that we'll also begin to crave someone who inspires us or challenges us to become the best possible version of ourselves. While these needs are ever-changing, they only begin to take root during this phase of the soul mate love.

This is the scary point when we begin to realize, Okay, this may not be what I want, but I don't know if I actually know what I want. At the reality phase of our soul mate relationship, we're likely to start being more honest with ourselves—not necessarily because we want to, or feel ready for the changes we may invite into our lives, but because it will steadily become impossible not to.

At that point we will start thinking more honestly about what it is we need from a partner and may begin to feel that we need someone who fully supports us, that we desire someone who helps us feel free, or even helps us find out more about who we are. While these questions are necessary, what we don't realize is we are still looking for someone else to help us feel a certain way about ourselves because we're still unable to do that, and it will actually help usher in our next relationship: the karmic.

I always ask clients, "What are your nonnegotiables?"—those core needs or desires that you're not willing to compromise. Sometimes it's that he's open to children, other times that he is a provider, or even great at personal care. Regardless of what these nonnegotiables are, if they are rooted in our core needs, they provide a great check-in point for us when we start a new relationship.

Using the nonnegotiables model lets us eliminate the months—or years—spent with someone who simply wants different things than we do, so that we're more clear up-front about what our needs are.

Even more concisely, I often will ask women to condense their list of nonnegotiables even further, to just one word. I compare this to a job description: If you were posting an ad for a life partner, which word would you use? Provider? Nurturer? Encourager? Protector? Being able to define our needs with one word lets us know what is most important to us in a relationship and allows us to focus on that. So maybe he breaks a few of the nonnegotiables, maybe there are long-distance issues to figure out, but if he fits our one word, then it may be worth it to see where the relationship can go.

All of these feelings and realizations are necessary because they begin to help us make the break from needing our soul mate to define us and our life path, and instead give ourselves the freedom to design it for ourselves.

This is when we start seeing the situation as it really is, and also when perhaps we stop trying so hard to make it fit. We don't stop trying because the love is gone, however, and that is just one reason why breaking up with our soul mate becomes as difficult as it does; it's always easier to end things with someone once the feelings are no longer there.

JUST BECAUSE THE RELATIONSHIP ENDS DOESN'T MEAN THE LOVE DOES

As we age and move through life, we realize that it's not that we really ever unlove someone but rather that love changes, as well as our need for it. Our soul mate is our first love, the one who gave love its meaning. That seems like everything we could want until we begin to ask ourselves what exactly *do* we want from this life. So this love doesn't actually go away, it doesn't die, and usually soul mates never have the kind of breakup where they hate each other. Instead, it's a slow realization that the love with a soul mate is a constant, it's curling up on the couch in front of a roaring fire, with our favorite book that we've read a thousand times.

Then we begin to understand that this love was simply comfortable, and while it was exactly what we needed to experience at the time, it wasn't actually going to help us continue on the path to become the people that we need to be in this life.

I don't love often but when I do, it's forever. One of my exes, a man I thought would be my happily-ever-after, ended up exiting my life in a tornado of consequences and self-realizations. At one point I thought that I no longer loved him, that maybe it was never love. Yet it's amazing what our ego can convince us of when it doesn't want to admit something.

Admitting to myself, even to him, that I still loved him was like setting myself free because sometimes the love doesn't die—but that doesn't necessarily mean the relationship is meant to continue, especially when only one person wants it.

In many ways, this phase of the soul mates makes me think of the comedy *Bride Wars* with Anne Hathaway and Kate Hudson, a cutesy movie about best friends who get into a duel when their weddings are accidentally scheduled on the same day. In the film, Anne Hathaway's character, Emma, breaks up with her fiancé at the altar, saying that he loves the person she was: the girl he fell in love with in college, not the grown woman she has since become. This sentiment echoes the feeling that many soul mates around the world have at the time things are beginning to crumble: "You're not in love with me, truly me, but only the idea of me."

It's difficult to distinguish why a love that we thought would last forever suddenly feels like maybe it was never really love. But the truth is that it was; the only thing that really changed was us. Our definition of love changes as we begin to know ourselves more deeply and as we become more aware of what our core needs and nonnegotiables are. The interesting aspect of this relationship is that it's almost because of its traditionalism that we become encouraged to grow, and not in fact the personal dynamics between ourselves and our soul mate.

Sometimes we don't know how much we want to fly until we feel like we are unable to; sometimes it takes someone pointing to a small box saying "fit here" for us to say hell no and make the choice to find what fits us best.

But in order to know how we need to be loved, we first need to be loved in all the ways we don't. This means that during this phase, not only do our core needs change from more socially based to helping our personal development, but we also start feeling like our idea of love changes as well. In the beginning, we often equate love with that happily-ever-after feeling of rings, white dresses, and promises of forever; but once we stop thinking of love in only a Disney romantic fashion, we can then start to explore the dynamics of an emotion that helps two people not just stay together forever, but stay in love forever as well.

Our soul mates love us with all that they have, but as a client of mine once said, "We can't keep going to the hardware store expecting to buy bread." The idea is the same for our relationships and the love we choose. In many ways we don't consciously choose our soul mates. Instead we fit together because of our upbringing, society, and even the comfort we give to each other, but that doesn't mean it's what we truly need. Just because someone loves you with all they have doesn't in fact mean it will fulfill what you truly need from a partner.

Our soul mates would never leave us, but that doesn't mean they can stay, either.

REALIZING IT'S OVER

Usually it feels like we grow apart from our soul mate at some point, that perhaps they are stuck on mile marker one while we're already at five. We begin to feel that the love is closing in on us, expecting too much from us, and so we begin to distance ourselves. In some ways these new ideas do challenge us, but instead of moving toward self-growth, we step away from our soul mate, to give up the person that we were when we were in a relationship with them. Because we never actually chose this relationship, the not-choosing becomes complicated.

We boomerang with them, coming and going because, while we love them, what we're struggling to put into words and accept is that it's not the love we need.

Beneath the surface, we will begin to meet our own darkness. We will feel guilt about parting with someone who only ever loved us; we will take on the breaking down of the relationship as a personal failure; and it's during this phase that we begin to ask what love truly is. We will doubt our decisions and wonder if we made the biggest mistake of our life.

We need to experience the darkness before we can get to the light, however. The darkness is what will permeate our next relationship, the karmic, for these very reasons.

To break up with our soul mate isn't just about ending a long-term relationship or walking away from someone we love; we must actually walk away from a life and a way of being. Regardless of who we are, or even if we're male or female, we all have a vision for our life, but this phase was one of conventionality, of fitting in.

To end our soul mate relationship is to make the decision to go against the mainstream, to break free from what we were supposed to do, and also to disappoint those we love the most.

In order to make the separation between ourselves and our soul mate, we have to be okay with being single once again, with dating, with getting married later in life. And we have to reconcile ourselves to the fact that the person we commit to will be different from the person we had pictured.

It takes going through all of our loves—the soul mates and the karmic passions—to fully learn and embody these lessons. This is where self-work takes seed, however, where we are finally given the chance not just to create our own lives, but also to discover what makes us happy.

Jamie has been married to the same man for almost twenty years and is just starting to figure that out. At this point, all she knows is the turmoil and unhappiness of the marriage; she's unable to even recognize what makes her happy. In one of our most recent conversations, she said, "I know I can do it, I know I could get through life, but I wonder if there is something more to it than just this."

I wanted to grab her through the phone and say, "Of course there's more to life than being unhappy!" but more than that, I wanted to tell her that we should never for one minute think that life is something simply to "get through." As we talked, she revealed that one of the deciding factors for her was her children: she didn't want them to have to go through what in her mind she's built up as the worst possible scenario—divorce.

More than any other type of love, our families and support systems figure heavily in this type of relationship, of course, because our soul mate is the person they want us to be with, and because we're doing what we are supposed to be doing: steadily following the blueprints for life that we were given as children, never really knowing if it was going to lead to ultimate happiness. Because of this, we often feel like a huge failure when we leave these relationships.

Our families usually have no problem telling us that we disappointed them or that "It's just a shame you two couldn't make it work, you were so perfect together," as if that is the problem; as if the connection and relationship between two people is a simple mathematical equation.

Knowing who we are is essential to knowing what type of love we need in order to flourish. While the lesson of understanding that our family's happiness does not in fact guarantee our own takes time to learn, ending things with our soul mate is where we begin to see that we have to grow beyond the expectations that others had for us if we are truly to feel fulfilled within this life. It may seem contradictory that in order for us to learn who we truly are, we have to stop being who our families want us to be. But in so many ways there is just no other option.

Some of us may have more supportive families than others, yet we will still need to stop making the "right" choices and instead start making choices that feel right.

At this phase of our life, we are just beginning to grow, just beginning to glimpse who we truly are, and at times it's scary. During this time, the best thing we can do is simply learn to trust ourselves: if something doesn't feel like it fits, if it's not right for us and the person it feels like we're becoming, then we don't need to find a reason, we only need to trust ourselves. We all look for logical reasons why something won't work. We like to say we have different interests, or we're going on different paths, but sometimes there is no reason that two people can't make it work—the only thing that really matters is that they're not meant to.

Admitting this truth to ourselves is difficult, though, and we often arrive at it only after multiple times of trying to make it work. It's a slow process of first waking up to the reality of the relationship and then becoming comfortable enough with the truth that we find there so that we can then speak it to our partner. Even when we do, it's likely that our partner won't accept it the first time around; they will refuse to end things, try to talk us back into being with them, or sometimes even use guilt.

Rarely do soul mates wake up to the truth of the relationship at the same time. There is always one who starts to grow and recognize that while the love itself is comfortable, it's not what they truly desire from a partner moving forward. Once we've accepted our truth, the only thing we can do is present it to our partner. The more uncertain we are about our decisions, the longer this relationship will actually take to end, so we can find closure and move on in our lives.

We have to realize during this process that we're not here to make choices that make others happy; we're not here to have things go according to someone else's plan. Ultimately, no one goes into a relationship expecting it to end and to hurt someone, but that doesn't mean it's not meant to happen. Pain can lead to lessons, to better understanding of ourselves and others.

While our karmic relationship is the one in which the most pain is shared from partner to partner, pain from a soul mate breakup is very deep because it makes us feel like we let down the world when we decided that this relationship wasn't for us.

But in the end, it's not about the rest of the world. It's not about society or even our families. It's about the shattered dreams that we have because we built up a certain relationship in our minds to be something that it's just not. In that case, not only is it ego we have to contend with because life is going differently than we had imagined—but it's also our hearts, because they tend to have a really hard time giving up on someone that we love, that we've built a dream around.

Maggie loves big. She has a big personality and an even bigger heart and wants to see the best in everyone, but she also believes in the impossible working out. She believes in those crazy love stories where two people find their way back to each other against all odds. So when her partner began to show signs of mental health problems and was refusing to get help, she found it hard to see reality, to see that maybe this relationship wasn't going to work and that it wasn't about trying harder, or sticking it out, but in seeing what was really happening in front of her. So she stayed; she stayed even though ultimately she wanted to go, not just because she wanted that big fourth-quarter love-game win but because she didn't know how to walk away from someone she loved.

Seeing reality is hard because even when we tell our partners that it's over, we might not yet be convinced ourselves. It might feel like we're trying something on for size, almost in an "I wonder if I wasn't with this person anymore, would I truly feel happier" kind of way. We get caught up in how to end things, how to move on, how to exist within a relationship that we never thought would end but that has, in fact, ended.

These dilemmas are also part of the process as well, however. At this stage, we still think that there is a right way and a wrong way to do anything, not yet understanding that the point is simply to just do it.

We have to commit ourselves to our happiness, and while later on in our development the meaning and vision of happiness shifts, at this stage it's almost like someone told us our entire life we could only shop for clothes at the local corner store and then one day we're brought to Target and it's overwhelming because there's so much more than we even realized was possible.

STEPPING INTO THE FIRE

Each one of us is a phoenix. Each one of us is meant to spread her beautiful strong wings, each one of us is meant to rise from the ashes and fly farther than we ever thought possible. But before we do that, we need to step into the fire.

Life is bigger than we can imagine at this point; there is more to all of this than just fitting in and playing nice. We have a bigger purpose than just marrying the people our families approve of, settling down, having children, and then essentially waiting to die without really ever truly having lived. But in order to actually grasp all that is possible, we need to be brave enough to reach out. We have to choose to let go of what we have, not knowing what is next. It means that we won't have all the answers. It means that ultimately we're going to have to jump not really knowing what it is that we are jumping into.

It's where we have to start trusting our own soul, our heart, and stop thinking that somehow everyone knows what we want better than we do ourselves.

After leaving our soul mate, we feel fired up about life, never really wanting to go back to fitting into that same tired worn-out box everyone expected us to live in. But that doesn't mean our lessons are over. It only means that this love is the starting point. Even if we ricochet back to it after our karmic love has decimated our lives, it's still just the start of what's to come. Our soul mates jump-start our hearts, they wake us up to those amazing feelings of love and desire, and it's the relationship in fact not working out that actually challenges us to start finding our own path in life.

No one leaves comfort unless they absolutely have to. No one decides to hurt someone unless it's absolutely necessary, and no one starts putting themselves first unless they get damn tired of pleasing everyone else.

The one aspect of this phase of the soul mate relationship is that even knowing it's not a perfect fit, we still go back and try again (hello, definition of insanity: doing the same thing repeatedly, expecting different results). Usually it's not until we've tried multiple times that we begin to have that definitive clarity that we need to actually end the relationship for good. A big part of this process is the lack of confidence many experience during this phase, which prohibits us from choosing a different life—yet the more confidence we acquire, the more we're able to take on the starring roles in our own lives.

Even knowing it's over, even in stepping away from fear, it still doesn't mean our soul mates are gone from our lives permanently. Rarely do we part ways with our soul mates and never speak again. Sometimes it's because we share a child together, but it can even just be that periodically we're drawn to reach out to them.

Though many years have passed since I was with my soul mate, recently I felt drawn to reach out to see how he was doing, which came as an odd surprise to him because the night before he had had a dream about me, a classic occurrence in soul mate connections. It wasn't that we were reconnecting or longed to be together, but that our souls were just doing a check-in; he told me about his life and how he's been growing, and I shared with him what was new with me.

Once we do end things with our soul mate, that physical intimacy boundary is never crossed again, and sometimes we can even enjoy them as one of our closest friends.

Soul mates have an important purpose in our life, but one of their greatest roles is being the first step in the journey to ourselves. We no longer need the identity, the comfort zone, story line, or even validation that they and the relationship provided.

It's up to us to let go when the time comes and to never look back, because the truth with any relationship is, if it was meant to work out, if it truly was your forever love, it would still be with you now—but it's not.

And not only is that okay, it's also exactly the way it's supposed to be. Of all the relationships that we enter into in our lives, only one is supposed to last into old age; only one is going to show you why it was never meant to work out with anyone else.

PART III

THE LESSON

We Can't Make Others Happy
Until We Are Happy

Inside each of us is a beat drumming in tune with our own unique rhythm. It's a voice that calls to us from the darkness, pulling us back to ourselves each time we begin to drift away from our essence. It can also take a lifetime, however, to tune in to this inner knowing and make the choice to listen to it. It's the choice to listen to the voice that tells us when something is meant for us, a voice that doesn't let us sleep soundly in the mundane but instead wakes us up to the spirit dancing inside of us.

Our soul mate is the one who creates the first connection to that inner voice because, in order to truly break free from this love and the comfort that it represents, we also have to be willing to follow a path that we never imagined existed. Soul mates are so deliciously comforting that when we first begin to experience the impossibility of the relationship and then move through the disintegration of the union, we often feel lost without it.

LEARNING TO ENJOY THE JOURNEY

For some, the lesson comes early on, as the relationship is ending—that fragile knowing that perhaps we might know more about who we are than we had previously thought, even if in the beginning it feels overwhelming and scary. The most important lesson we learn from this love is that we can't make others happy before we are happy ourselves, and so when we remove the external validation that this love provided, there are always some mixed feelings. Suddenly the world seems so much bigger, so much more unpredictable than we had believed it to be!

Often the lesson presents itself not so much from our partner—although they may make the classical remark that they are disappointed in us because of our choice to have a life that is different from the one they imagined they'd have with us—but instead from our families or even our friends. To end things with our soul mate is to ultimately tell our parents, our best friends, that they don't know better than we do what makes us happy, what we ultimately need, what truly defines love for us.

We have to break away from that ego base that formed during childhood and adolescence, when we were growing and maturing into a role already shaped for us.

So many of our relationship choices go back to ego, because the ego controls our beliefs about what is normal, even to what level we get to know who we truly are. As long as we're making choices from ego—"I should do this"—then we're not letting our inner self, our soul, decide. Which means we're also not truly getting to know who we really are.

The primary obstacle to breaking free is that however much we think we know what we want and what makes us happy at this stage, we simply don't. Even if we have ended and had time to process the relationship with our soul mate, we're still not certain of how we need to be loved. Instead, we are only just becoming aware of what we *don't* need. Yet this love still served a purpose, even if that purpose was only to learn that the relationship had to end. This experience taught us how to love another person and learn what it felt like to build a life with someone. So ultimately, while this relationship has ended, it far from failed.

When it comes to love, we often see the ending of a relationship as failure: We failed. Our partner failed to make us happy. But in truth, no relationship truly fails. It's only that the majority of relationships are supposed to end, something we rarely see on the silver screen.

One of the few movies to illustrate this concept—that happily-ever-after isn't necessarily when the couple says "I do," is the 2017 romcom *Home Again* starring Reese Witherspoon. In this modern love story, Alice moves away to her father's home in L.A. after separating from her long-time husband, and ends up having three adorable twenty-somethings move into her guesthouse. The film goes through the withering end of her relationship with her husband, even after he professes his love for her and wants to make it work, as well as a casual and fun booty-call relationship with one of the younger men.

The last scene of this film isn't a wedding, or even a proposal, however, but Reese's character, Alice, sitting at the dinner table casually laughing and talking with her children, her ex, and the three younger men, who have become family friends.

It was an ending, but it was also a beginning. In many ways this is what our soul mate love often is; it's not really a failure, it's not the fault of one or both partners, but rather the love and the purpose of the relationship changed from a romantic-forever feeling into a familial relationship or friendship. Not every love is meant to stay in our lives, but because our soul mates are often those we have children with, the love that is shared tends to be one where the love outlasts the romance.

Yet in this film, Reese's character, Alice, ultimately had to travel through various circumstances in order to truly find what makes her happy and to build the life that she truly wanted. She didn't follow the wants of her children—to move back to New York City—nor did she follow the desires of any of the men in her life. Instead she stuck to her boundaries, knew what she deserved, and in the end she chose her happiness above all others'.

Choosing our own happiness is what ultimately defines the journey to self, which one of my clients, Addie, learned firsthand in her relationship. She met her significant other at a time in her life when she was just starting to open to the possibility of love. Addie was realistic about love but still believed that happily-ever-after was the same as lasting forever, and so when her partner started to lie to her, to sneak around and ultimately betray her, she felt torn.

Should she try to work it out, should she leave, was the dilemma she was faced with. It wasn't that she didn't love him or believe in love itself, but she didn't feel she could honor who she was and her boundaries about what she deserved while staying with him. So Addie, in the end, chose herself; she chose her happiness and walked away from a man who she was incredibly in love with because she refused to sacrifice herself for another.

TUNING IN TO OUR INNER VOICE

We all have a voice inside of us, one that isn't a part of ego but that is connected to our soul and our heart. It's the one that guides our intuition and feels like it speaks our true needs. Often, however, we get used to ignoring this voice.

We grow accustomed to talking ourselves out of what we feel are our deepest truths because of logic, friends, family, or even the story lines we've built up. To do this, though, we must have become comfortable with allowing others to voice their opinions about how we are messing up our lives or making a wrong choice.

While even those who love us the most have good intentions, at times their words still cut us or at the very least make us doubt our choices regarding our soul mate. They don't do this out of spite or even a conscious desire to control us, but rather because once we deviate from the life plan of those around us, we are seen as a safety risk to the entire system.

This system is the one telling us we can only grow up and get married; that says we have to wear white, or wait six (who are we kidding, three) dates before having sex for the first time. So in learning that we can't make others happy before we ourselves are happy, we also are declaring that the system is wrong; that we don't want what we were told we were supposed to have. In those moments, while our breath catches in our throats and our knees tremble, we're taking that first step to knowing ourselves.

When I met Theresa, she had a list of rules a mile long about what a potential man had to possess and a time line for dating, sex, saying I love you, and even moving in. So far, that list hadn't gotten her much more than a few heartbreaks, and so we worked on why the list had become so important to her. Over the course of a few months, she became aware that this list was based on what she thought would make her happy, what she thought she should do. No surprise, then, that it very much held the thoughts and opinions of those closest to her.

But to actually get to that third and final love, we have to be prepared to do things differently, no matter how hard it might be. So we began focusing on what made her happy—as simple as that. We spoke about what type of qualities were actually important and why letting go of control would end up actually bringing her closer to what she needed.

Theresa is now living with a man twenty years younger who remodeled their home shortly after moving in, and they just returned from an incredible vacation to Italy. Together they travel, go out, laugh, and have so much incredible sex that she feels decades younger—but this man, the one who cooks her dinner and gives her foot rubs after a long day, doesn't fit a single one of the original rules on her list.

Sometimes we need to throw out the rules in order to find what actually fits.

In so many ways this story is similar to the 1998 hit film, and one of my favorites, *How Stella Got Her Groove Back*, starring Angela Bassett and Taye Diggs and based on the best-selling novel by Terry McMillan. The movie begins with Stella, played by Bassett, wanting to break free from her routine life by taking a spontaneous trip to Jamaica. Of course, once there she meets adorable Winston, played by Diggs, a local man more than a decade her junior who challenges every rule Stella ever lived by.

During the course of the movie, we see Stella surrender her attachment to the opinions of others, as well as her own inner story about the kind of man she should spend her life with—something many of us struggle with, without even realizing we're the ones holding ourselves back from love.

At the end of the film, she chooses happiness and, more important, herself. She learns to let go of the rules and preconceived notions of how to find true love.

Ending things with our soul mate begins our journey toward knowing ourselves. In many ways, however, because the focus with our soul mate is on finding the courage to end the relationship and getting through everyone's disappointment about it ending, we have yet to learn some of the hardest things about ourselves, and this is why the karmic relationship is frequently the next love that we encounter. While we begin to get to know ourselves and test our wings after this love, seeing what makes us happy in this life, what we haven't realized is that we can't truly know who we are until we go deeper and address the events that have created the person we thought we had to be.

At this stage, we are actually preparing ourselves, usually unknowingly, for our karmic love. We think we're free, we feel free, but all the while we're still handcuffed to our insecurities, our misgivings, our wounds, and our projections about how we think we need to operate in this world now that we're separate from our soul mate. It's not that we're entirely blind to reality, but at this stage our view is much more simplistic. After all, we've only experienced one of the three types of relationships that are meant to come into our lives and challenge us to the point that we can finally make the choice to change ourselves.

But as with any journey, it's not the destination or even where we'll end up down the road that matters, but rather the moment we find ourselves in. As we are moving away from our soul mate and starting to figure out who we are, we may begin to try on new personas or qualities. This is because while with our first love we were focused on trying to be so conventional or even domestic, now the pressure to be perfect in these areas is no longer a weight on our shoulders. There is more room for us to explore other aspects of self.

We might find ourselves out dancing until three a.m., doing shots with the cute neighbor downstairs, or even by ourselves swearing off love indefinitely, telling ourselves that maybe we're just not meant for what it seems so many have.

After our soul mate relationship, we may go through a phase of trying to prove to others that we in fact *do* know what makes us happy and that we *do* know who we are. In part this is because while in the soul mate relationship, we began to identify those needs that were not being met, and now that we are out of that relationship, we feel compelled to explore our own inner divine essence that sets us apart from anyone else. Add to this the fact that, because we are usually younger when this love ends, we also feel the need to explore life more before settling down immediately into a relationship. But there is a big difference between using experiences with others as a distraction and using those experiences as a way to help ourselves grow.

DOUBT ISN'T CODE FOR "TRY AGAIN"

Often, we want to be sure before we end things with a partner, almost like we're hoping to have things get as bad as they can so that we can be positive that breaking up is the right thing to do. Instead, we have to learn that uncertainty is okay, it doesn't mean that the relationship is meant to last or that we are wrong for what we were feeling.

Ultimately, we're more scared of where to go from here than we are of returning to what we know doesn't work.

It's because of this that we sometimes have another go at the relationship, or start to doubt ourselves enough that we begin to wonder if others really do know us better than we do. We also may begin to miss how easy things were, especially if we begin to date or open ourselves to new people and experiences. It may be that we'll start to see that the connection with our soul mate was special and think that should be a good reason to go back to them and try again.

One important question to consider is, is the doubt coming from fear or from love? Are we scared of making a mistake, scared of moving forward, of being single? Or are we doubting because we love this person so much, because it seems like they're trying, and that maybe this rough spot was meant so we both could grow closer?

In the end, if the doubt keeps resurfacing, this usually means that it is fear that is holding us in this relationship. Eventually, we come to realize that nothing about the relationship is changing and instead it is we ourselves who are changing. The only difference between the ending of this love now and a few months or years out is that from time to time we will miss the comfort and knowingness this relationship provided. I've known soul mates who have taken a decade or more to split up. One of my clients, Jess, finally realized twelve years and two children later that the love she kept running back to was also slowly killing her.

Jess kept going back time and time again, even moving out and moving back in, because it seemed that maybe no one would ever love her as much as this man did. But she was also petrified of being single, well, not just single—"alone forever" was often what she would talk about. So she kept returning to him when the fear got to be too much, until she finally had a realization one night that maybe there was nothing truly wrong with her ex, maybe there was nothing really wrong in the relationship, but that all it really was for her was a comfort zone.

If she never left permanently, she would never know what was waiting on the other side of that fear.

Perhaps some would say it sounds like an extreme, but for many of us that lulling ease is so addictive because with it, we never have to experience uncertainty or fear; we never have to actually let life be what it's meant to be instead of making it what we think it should be. And of course we never have to actually take the time and make the commitment to find out who we truly are.

The interesting thing about soul mates is that the relationship never really changes. Whether it's the first go-around or twelve years and two kids later, it always feels the same—but so do the problems. For Jess, the comfort that she sought for so long turned into her cage. When we spoke during our very first call, I can still remember hearing Jess sobbing and saying, "I don't know how we became this, I don't know why I can't just leave."

At times we tend to romanticize these moments, thinking that because we can't leave someone, it must mean that we're meant to be with them; but often it's just that we're using them to escape ourselves—and the work life asks us to do in order to continue to grow, explore, and become the best possible version of ourselves.

Ending our soul mate love is us saying that we're ready to grow and discover who we truly are.

#AUTHENTICALLYLIVINGMYBESTLIFE

"Living my best life" is an expression that seems to have caught like wildfire over recent years, even making it to hashtag status with #livingmybestlife. Yet in truth, many of those shots that we post on Instagram aren't necessarily us living our best life. Just because we travel, do yoga, meditate, eat vegetarian or vegan, it doesn't actually mean we're living our best life. Just because we can post that new kitchen remodel or a nap on the beach on a lazy Sunday doesn't actually mean we're living our best life, because "living my best life" isn't something that can be defined via a photo for the masses to see, or that can be exploited superficially. It's something you feel internally.

In Jess's case, she hadn't just lost her essence; she had never found it. In addition to leaving her soul mate relationship, she had the daunting task of trying to find out who she was while also raising two small humans and working, all at the same time. Yes, this was her path, but just because we're meant to experience something in order to learn from it doesn't mean we actually need to keep suffering.

The art and practice of letting go is another phrase often mistakenly used as a way to release ourselves from something. But letting go actually means that we let go of our control, let go of that mental picture or story line, and instead choose to let life, let the divine, show us the way.

This is what it means to find ourselves, to leave our soul mate and comfort zone, and ultimately to give ourselves the freedom to discover what #livingmybestlife means for each of us. It means that we get to wander aimlessly in flea markets or crystal shops in search of treasures; we get to try out different styles of clothing and travel solo; we get to be the authors of our own goddamn story.

As impossible as leaving is, staying is even worse. It's those moments where we know that it's not just a matter of a failed relationship; it's a matter of not being able to be our true selves or even discover what that means.

And so we have to learn the hard way sometimes that #livingmy-bestlife doesn't always mean being in a relationship.

SEX IS NEVER CASUAL BETWEEN SOUL MATES

While we can learn many important lessons in the on-again, off-again relationship with our soul mate, we don't actually get to begin the heavy lifting of finding out who we truly are as long as we're involved with them—and yes, that even includes the occasional hookup as well. It's a hard world out there, especially when it comes to satisfying our sexual desires and needs. But as long as we choose to exchange energy with someone we know we won't have a future with, we will also remain stuck in the past. For Jess, not letting go of her soul mate in this way resulted in the birth of one child, and then two, and the longer they took to separate, the more difficult it became.

It's normal. Many of us want to have sex with someone we've been with before, whom we love and whom we also know we can enjoy it with. But sex in itself does not make a relationship, and it also still ties us energetically to an ex, sapping energy and preventing us from actually moving forward with our lives.

For soul mates, there is no casual sex.

The longer we engage in the occasional booty call with our soul mate, the less likely we are to put ourselves out there for our next love—and there's also the risk of being permanently attached to them through the birth of a child.

In Cecilia's case, she and her soul mate had broken up. They were done. She had moved out, and while she would tell anyone who would listen that she didn't want her ex back, there was still that soft spot for him. So when they started texting more and he asked if he could come by to see her because he missed her—she said yes. Once again she thought that maybe the outcome would be different; and then again, even if it wasn't—well, it had been six long months since she'd last had sex and she was craving that physical intimacy!

A month later, she had a little pink plus sign show up on a pregnancy stick, and thought even then that a baby might make things different. Even though she had moved out a year before and even though she knew this man and she had all sorts of reasons for not trying, that small part of her that held out hope still thought maybe this time . . .

Maybe this time it will be different.

Yet all that happened was she got to weave in and out of several more years and just as many breakups with him until she finally learned that it was never going to work.

CRYING ON THE KITCHEN FLOOR

I'm a crier. It's just who I am. But never have I sobbed like I did when my relationship with my soul mate ended. My heart was truly broken. I literally would crumple on the kitchen floor in front of the sink and sob uncontrollably. Not only was my heart hurting, but I had no idea why I had to go through this, and none of it seemed fair.

I wish I could say that I was able to pull myself together in front of my girls, but so many times my little one would come and lie next to me saying, "It's okay, Mommy, I cry too sometimes." Sometimes she'd actually cry with me.

But it was in these moments on the kitchen floor that I found the most important tool I would need on the journey to finding myself—the strength to get back up and keep going.

We can live a better life and be a better version of ourselves after ending the soul mate relationship, but it will never be our best life or best version of ourselves because we still need to make that journey through the dark underworld of everything that we kept hidden during this phase in our lives, even from ourselves.

Living our best life isn't the pics we post on vaca with no cares in the world, but rather that quiet self-assuredness that is present, even within the most chaotic of times.

To live our best life means being happy with ourselves, to not just like but *love* the shit out of who we are. It's living unapologetically—not necessarily carefree because, let's be real, life is hard, there's no easy button or way out of getting our hearts broken, losing jobs, or having the world turn upside down. So, living our best life is learning that if we are at our personal best, then life feels that way regardless of whether we're heading into parent-teacher conferences, boarding a plane to our next adventure, or ecstatically kissing the love of our life until time disappears.

It's the relationship with our soul mate that indirectly and unconsciously jump-starts that journey for us to figure that out for ourselves.

When we are happy with ourselves, we are at peace. It's not that we're not striving for more or have become complacent; but it does mean accepting ourselves as we are in this moment and surrendering to whatever reality is presenting itself. To end the time of romantic love with our soul mate is to finally find the courage to say, "I love you, but I love who I want to become even more."

The minute we actually decide to put our happiness before that of others—and stick with it—we open the doors to discover what happiness truly means for us.

The thing is, living our best life is a commitment; it's a process and a promise to our soul to never accept less than we know we deserve. And in order to feel we deserve something, we need to feel worthy and happy with ourselves. This is partly why we enter into the karmic relationship after our soul mate: even if we're unconsciously aware of it, we don't feel good about ourselves.

Until we heal, we'll keep bleeding on those who had nothing to do with our wounds. Until we accept ourselves as we are, who we are, without judgment or prejudice, then we will continually surround ourselves with those who validate the negative or limiting self-talk that we have subscribed to all our lives.

Knowing who we are is a complex system of being at home with our own dreams, our likes and dislikes, aspirations, motivations, and triggers (things that set us off). Even once we truly heal from all that we have experienced up until this point and those wounds have transformed to nothing more than light-pink scars, we will forever be triggered from time to time. Yet each time we are triggered, we can go deeper into healing, which then translates into that much deeper knowing of our soul as well.

In order to live our best life and be our best possible self, we need to believe that we are worthy of our deepest desires for ourselves, our lives, and our relationships. It's knowing that just because our parents' marriage didn't work out doesn't mean ours won't; it's knowing that just because our father left us doesn't mean every man is destined to; and it's believing that we are worthy of the love that everyone says we are crazy to believe actually exists.

As we separate from our soul mate and more time passes, we also feel like we have to align less with our families or social circles that have surrounded us. It's to ultimately know that regardless of how happy everyone else was that we were going to marry our high school sweetheart or the sweet girl from the right family and neighborhood, ultimately it didn't align with our truth. To be aligned with our truth is to go one step further than just being our best selves.

The sole purpose of our soul mate love is to end—not fail, but end—so that we may be presented with the valuable lessons that we are in such desperate need of, and so that we can finally move forward in our lives.

The lesson above all others is that we have to be the creator of our own life; we have to be the artist of our own masterpiece. If we were to sit down and create a piece of art, we wouldn't hand the paintbrush off to our mother, sister, or neighbor! Instead, we'd sit and dream; we'd see what wanted to reveal itself on the canvas.

This is the experience of living: we have to experiment, we have to take the time to try different things just so that we may know for sure whether or not they fit us, whether or not they are meant, ultimately, to be a part of the masterpiece that we call our lives.

LOVE IS A VEHICLE FOR SELF-GROWTH

Love is not just love in itself, but a vehicle for self-growth. The sooner we accept this reality, the sooner we can begin to open up to life and all of the possibilities it has in store for us. Love never comes the way we think it will or how we expect it will; instead, it shows up announced as a sweet lover sliding between black satin sheets, whispering in our ear all the things that create shivers and goosebumps on our skin even if we never imagined someone would ever say them to us.

To view love as a way to grow and experience life means that it will never fail. We don't need someone else to approve of it or say we're doing the right thing. We don't have to hold fear, thinking, *What if it ends,* because an ending often isn't the worst-case scenario. The worst-case scenario can be hanging on much too long and not experiencing what life is trying to bring you.

There were moments of heartbreak so deep for myself that I felt like I couldn't breathe; and worse, I didn't see a way out. I didn't care about anything else in that moment except that the person I loved wasn't there next to me. I couldn't even think of moving out from beneath my comforter.

It wasn't just that my heart was broken but that I didn't want to feel better because I didn't want to be able to be okay, to be great, and to live without him. Being brokenhearted became my story line; I didn't care at all about the reason why or the ultimate purpose.

But sometimes our only option is to call "Bullshit!" on ourselves. We have to be the ones to decide to grow, to change, and to accept whatever reality is in that moment. So I got tired of being brokenhearted, of holding myself while I fell asleep whispering to myself, "You are loved." Ultimately, I got tired of myself and so I started to search, hell, *dig* for anything that would make sense of what I was feeling.

And it was in that moment that I first began to commit to my growth and whoever I would become in the future because of what I was experiencing then.

PARENTING WITH A SOUL MATE

It is always difficult to end the soul mate relationship and begin the next chapter of our lives, but those cases in which children are present can be even more difficult because there will always be that connection. This means we have to be more mindful, more deliberate.

We have to get to the place where we can look at our soul mates with gratitude for what they brought into our lives, for the love experienced. At the same time, we have to also know that this love that was so comfortable is, in fact, now holding us back from experiencing the next phase of life and love.

Our romantic relationship has to transition to a platonic one because, while we want to be healthily present parents for our kids, we don't want to confuse them with questions such as, Are Mommy and Daddy together this week or not?

Ultimately, though, while this journey is about love, it's also about truth. The moment we realize that is also the moment where we begin to no longer repeat the pattern.

Cecilia now realized she had signed on for a lifetime of coparenting with a man that she loved, that she wished things could be different with, yet knew all the same that they would never be. During those several years in which they both tried to make it work, she had moments of thinking that things were wonderful—until he once again cheated on her, crashing her hopes that anything would be different. Cheating is a coward's way out of a relationship, but it's also what often occurs when we try to make a relationship work that isn't meant to—for either a man or a woman. Sometimes we cheat, subconsciously wanting to get caught and hoping our partner will be the one to end it so we don't have to. Sometimes it's just a clumsy attempt to start a new story before we've finished the one we're currently on.

Regardless of the reason why, it's never about the fact someone cheated, but rather about the reason behind it. For Cecilia, she knew that he wasn't fully invested in her, she knew that he loved someone else, but she also knew that his loyalty to their child was strong and so sometimes she used that as a way to try to bring his focus back to the relationship and make it work.

They went on like this for years until finally she got tired of having her own heart broken and made the choice to step back into only a coparent role. Once she made that choice, they both had to figure out what that meant, they had to renegotiate the boundaries and learn how to solve problems with sex, and also how to be happy for each other when they started dating other people.

To parent with a soul mate is to accept that the edges or boundaries may be messy for a while. It may mean that we have to constantly be firm in how friendly we are with them, and whether we ask them to support us as a coparent or as a romantic partner.

Soul mates can coparent, but only once they have instilled healthy boundaries within the relationship.

A perfect example of this is *The Single Moms Club*, a 2014 movie by Tyler Perry. The movie begins by introducing us to five very different and, in some ways, very opposite women who have one thing in common: they are all single moms. After their children are involved in an incident at school, the mothers are asked to plan an event together.

Despite their differences, each woman has faced a challenge with the men in their lives, particularly with boundary-setting. From dealing with controlling exes to less-than-perfect fathers, each mother has carried an often relatable burden of motherhood.

Through their shared experiences and camaraderie, they are able to help one another not only set better boundaries, but also feel happier and healthier. When we understand that boundaries are essential to our well-being rather than acts of selfishness, we can then start to be an advocate for ourselves and for our children.

We will always be family with our soul mates with whom we share a child, but that doesn't mean this romantic relationship is a healthy one, or fosters our self-growth. It simply means, again, as part of your soul family, you agreed to raise this child together because of the lessons that this process represents, not because you're supposed to try to make it work for the next eighteen years until he or she has graduated from high school.

It's also about knowing we're worthy of happiness too.

BEING OKAY WITH NOT BEING OKAY

Leaving behind the soul mate romantic phase means that we're committing to this journey even if we don't know where it will lead and even if we're scared. It means that we know comfort and growth are not the same thing, and that regardless of how we hoped the relationship would play out, we're accepting that it is not the one that will lead us to our best selves. While we love our soul mates deeply, we can't live our best possible lives with them.

A love that doesn't trigger us will never be able to help us grow. In other words, we need that friction in order to continue being polished. Once we absorb our lessons from our soul mate love and move on, we're ready to explore what truly makes us happy. We've learned that in order to bring any good to those who matter most to us, we first need to be good to ourselves.

The truth is, we accept relationships that mirror how we feel about ourselves. So to be able to say that our happiness matters is to begin the journey of defining what happiness *on our own terms* even means, knowing that the only person we're doing it for is ourselves. Until we can authentically separate from our soul mate and those whose approval we sought for so long, we will never truly move on.

We will never truly know what love is until we begin to learn who we truly are.

The Second Love, Our Karmic Partner

THE ONE WE WISHED WAS RIGHT

PART I

THE DREAM

This Time I'll Get It Right

There are times in life we become so focused on not doing things the same way, on leaving the past behind, that we begin what we think will be a new chapter before we've actually dealt with all the reasons why things went sour the last time.

We begin this new path before we actually deal with ourselves, before we learn to recognize those triggers that remind us of past trauma, and, of course, before we even know fully who we are.

Our second love begins with great intentions, but because we haven't entirely made a break from our patterns and taken time to be alone and understand our own personal why, we end up choosing a relationship with a karmic partner to help teach us.

Whether or not we acknowledge it, each of us does have our own personal why: the reasons we make the choices that we do, as well as the reasons we choose the relationships that we do. At this stage, we might not even be aware of our why. We might say that this person makes us feel good, or they are different, even exciting—these are common ways to describe the connection we feel with this new karmic love.

But it's not the same as our authentic why.

Our why takes into account the soul-to-heart connection, the reason we choose one path over another in life—and in our love life. It's the difference between "We have fun together" and "He helps me constantly want to be better." I've even heard men simply say, "My why? For marrying my wife? Easy, I knew I didn't want to live a day without her."

In the beginning, we're not aware that we haven't fully healed from our soul mate. There may be issues that linger: we may still lack a sense of self-worth, or familial and social conditioning may still color our views of love and relationships.

FALLING IN LOVE WITH THE IMAGE

Because we enter into karmic love not fully healed from our experiences with our soul mate, this karmic passion will not be the happily-ever-after we are seeking. When our soul mate relationship ended, we felt disillusioned about love. We wondered: If this wasn't real, what is? Does love even exist? It becomes difficult to imagine a different person being able to do for us what our soul mate couldn't. Will we ever be able to trust again, to love again, and to believe in the magic that we thought was gone forever?

Even so, we are not ready to confront the work we need to do within ourselves. Karmic love exists to teach us everything that we are still trying to avoid. Our level of self-awareness, however, is not deep enough to understand this and so we fall in love with the image we project onto our partner.

When we meet our second love, our karmic partner, very often we are swept away; we may even experience love at first sight. We become fixated on this new love, thinking that not only are we finally doing things differently but that this love will actually heal us, will help us become the people that we have always wanted to be or see ourselves as being.

We fall in love with all of the qualities that we *want* to see in them.

We also tend to fall in love with what we want to see in ourselves, without understanding that we're only using them as a way to make ourselves feel better—to avoid that hard work of learning who *we* are.

Evonne came to me because she couldn't understand why the opinions of others, especially her sisters, were so important to her—to the extent that she began to doubt her decisions and feelings about her relationship choices.

She grew up in a very tight-knit family, and worked with them as well: rarely was there a waking moment when some sister wasn't trying to tell her what she should do. She felt trapped, and only truly felt she could be herself when she was in a different state; she even hoped to move away eventually.

Yet this posed another problem: her sisters didn't want her to move.

So Evonne's relationship choice actually ended up being about the feeling of freedom that she felt when she was far away from home and family. She lives in Colorado but travels frequently to the

East Coast for work. While there, she met Tony and fell completely in love. Not only does she feel more at home on the coast, she feels free because she's away from her family and the pressure and opinions that suffocate her.

As we begin the early phase of the relationship with our karmic lover, we are still carrying many of the same needs and desires that we had with our soul mate. We're still thinking about some variation of traditional romance, including marriage, a home, and children. We're still concerned about whether or not our family will like the new person and how we will be seen by others once they know we are together.

Very often we choose our karmic partner because they exhibit qualities we want for ourselves: maybe they are extremely good-looking or buff; maybe they are "bad boys" when we are tired of being the "good girl"; maybe they are rich or live an extravagant lifestyle, all qualities we may envy or want for ourselves at the time. We also may choose them because they just make us feel better about ourselves: they validate our desires and our feelings.

Because we had the courage to leave our soul mate and the cycle we perpetuated with them, we also feel the high from the strength it took to leave. Now we want something completely different. This time we're not just trying to fulfill the fairy tale; this time we're not just staying with the mother or father of our children. This time we're making a choice for *us*, or so it seems. And for the honeymoon period with our new karmic lover, we feel like we made it, as though we've escaped any actual self-growth at all before falling in love again.

This time around, we are determined to do things differently. We're also steadfast in the idea that no matter what, this time we're not going to fuck it up like we did last time. In many ways, we're not actually looking at this love as one more stepping stone to our forever love, but instead as the person we've been working our way toward all along.

There is usually a cosmic magic to the meeting of our karmic partner. We might walk by each other and simply say hello, igniting a whirlwind romance, or maybe get paired together at work, or get our coffee orders mixed up at the local coffee shop.

In my case, it was love at first sight. I was eighteen, barely out of high school, with a head full of dreams and a wild spirit. So when I casually began walking down a darkened section of the local boardwalk with my group of friends in tow, I headed right for this man, almost as if my soul knew he would be there.

He was a year older, and in his white T-shirt and black jeans looked every bit the part of Danny Zuko from *Grease*. With my blond hair and sweet smile, I was more than willing to play his Sandy to whatever drama ensued from that first night.

I was caught up with his stories of being an engineering major and looking every bit the six-foot-tall wholesomeness of a man raised in the heartland. I was hooked and there was no going back.

Before I met him, I had dreams of being different, of traveling, of what I would study in college, but suddenly this relationship became my main focus. I was addicted not just to the powerful love that came at me out of nowhere, the dozens of roses he'd always send me, the image he projected to the outside world, but also how he made sense once again of a story line that I had thought I'd given up hope on.

The one of falling in love and living happily ever after.

CLEARING OUR KARMIC-LOVE DEBT

The nature of karmic love is that there is in fact karma that needs to be played out and balanced in this relationship.

We tend to think of karma as being only negative or something that will happen to us in retaliation for bad behavior. The symbol for karma, however, is the circle: what goes around, comes around. Karma itself is neither positive nor negative but only necessary. We are the ones who attach the ideas of good or bad to events in our life based on how we feel, without understanding that the moments that brought us to our knees were just as necessary as those memories of smiling and laughing with friends.

As long as we are living beings on earth, we all have karma to be cleared.

Sometimes the karma is from past lives. For example, if we were an angry or mean person in our previous life and didn't treat our loved ones well, then in this lifetime we would be on the receiving end of that energy so we could learn how it felt and thus end that destructive pattern of behavior. In this sense, it's not just karma; it's a karmic wound that is being healed.

This is not about us deserving what we experience, but about learning the lesson in it.

There is no good reason why people hurt others, there's no justification for betrayal or lack of integrity—but there is always a lesson we can learn from it. We choose the lens we see through. Is an event happening *to* us or *for* us? With this new lens, we can shift from a victim mentality to being able to take something away from it that would make us stronger, wiser, and more confident.

In karmic relationships, many of us are learning similar lessons and clearing the karma of not speaking up for ourselves, of being the doormat, being afraid to be alone, or wanting to be rescued. So we enter into these relationships not realizing that the purpose for them was not to last forever in and of themselves, but to clear the karmic debt that we came into this life with.

Just as soul mates travel together in soul families across time, karmic loves are those that we had unresolved issues with in a previous lifetime so we get another go-round in this lifetime. Aren't we lucky?

I smile as I remember shouting into the phone to one lover, "Is there anything else we have to do in this lifetime? Because I don't want to see you in another! If there's anything left to do to one another or say or work on, I want to do it now because I don't want to have to do this again!"

I laugh now, but it really speaks to the pain of our karmic loves. If we don't want to have to repeat the lessons, we have to make the most of what we're given so that we can clear out the debt.

If we look at karma not just as a debt to be balanced out, but as a way for us to learn, grow, and raise our awareness, then we can see that the more karma we clear in each love, in each lifetime, the higher our soul ascends.

In this moment, though, it's about finding our truth, standing up for ourselves, and making the choice to leave behind the patterns and approach our relationships differently.

While karma is most often associated with previous lifetimes, it's also accumulated within this one as well. So our karmic love may come in to clear those abandonment issues that we acquired as a child, or to be the mirror of emotional unavailability so that we learn to be more vulnerable in love moving forward. It's about absorbing the lessons, growing because of it, and then making the choice to operate from our higher self rather than our wounded self.

While karma is about what we clear, it's also about what we create.

DON'T FORGET TO TAKE YOUR BRAIN WITH YOU

In the last year of my Polish grandmother Babci's life, I visited her often in the hospital, sometimes painting her nails or bringing her lavender aromatherapy oils, but always talking with her.

She had developed Alzheimer's before my marriage was over and so I made the choice to not tell her, but like most grandmothers, she seemed to know anyway. One day in particular, when we were sitting on the edge of her hospital bed in the warm February sun, she squeezed my hand a little bit and told me that next time I fell in love to not forget to take my brain with me.

I had to love my Babci because she knew; she knew I had a hard time seeing the realities of love through the rose-tinted glasses I wore. I'll never forget her words to me that day and how important they truly are for all of us.

With our karmic partner, the feeling of love and attraction is so instant that it barely leaves any room for reflection, for taking time to evaluate if our goals and desires align in a healthy way. Instead, usually for both people, it becomes about the other person and the feelings they give us. This relationship isn't necessarily a rebound from our first love, our soul mate, but it is our chance to feel validation once again.

While many people, myself included, would say that they were beginning to grow during this time and that they weren't the same person they were while with their soul mate, in reality we haven't taken the time to know who we are. Once again we end up defining ourselves through someone else. Only now, instead of dreaming and planning with our soul mate, we're dreaming and planning with our karmic partner. There are definitive differences present; however, we either choose to ignore them or are so engrossed in the highs of love that we aren't consciously aware of them.

At this point we haven't yet clearly defined who we are apart from a romantic relationship, which is then reflected in the choices we end up making.

Very often there will be signs early on in the relationship, present even in the earliest phase, that the relationship isn't truly healthy or likely to last long-term. Sometimes it's that our partner cheats on us, or they begin to raise their voice, maybe even grabbing us during a heated argument. It's an addictive love that even from the beginning feels deliciously overwhelming, and so for those reasons, we either ignore the signs or explain them away.

It might be jealousy about social media or an ex, or it might sneak in more subtly through the gifts of clothing or hair appointments that seem loving and sweet, all the while exhibiting signs of control. But this time we're determined to get it right, and so we make excuses, we forgive, and we let ourselves continually be swept up in the throes of love, never stopping to wonder if this relationship is the one that we should be putting so much effort into.

One important motivating factor for this phase of our romantic journey is the fear of being alone.

While it first surfaced in our decision to leave our soul mate relationship, it still colors how soon—and with whom—we get into a romantic relationship afterward.

For our second love, the dream is that not only will we get it right but that we'll still live happily ever after. We'll still be able to control who our hearts fall for and we'll still be able to have the life that we had envisioned. We look to this partner in many ways to control us, to have a strong personality and tell us what we can or can't do so that we get a free pass from actually making these choices for ourselves. Perhaps we move to be around them because they want us near them, or we stop hanging out with friends because they don't think they are a good influence on us.

Maybe we change jobs or even our religious affiliation because we believe that we made a decision together, when all we're really doing is trying to become more like the person that we think our partner would want us to be.

Jada first reached out to me because she couldn't get over her ex. Not just in an "Oh, I wish I was still with him kind of way," but she had become obsessed, stalking him on social media, fabricating reasons to reach out to him, and even rehearsing texting conversations she might have with him. It wasn't just that she couldn't get over him, but for so many years this man defined the woman that she was. Any confidence she felt in herself was solely attached to his attention or to the fact that he had chosen her.

Once the relationship ended, Jada couldn't let go: not only did she still have feelings for him, but she had no idea who she was and she was terrified of being single the rest of her life. She said that she'd be happier with him, that life would be better with him, not realizing that she herself had placed the key to her happiness in his hands— and when he left, he took it with him.

We have to understand that during this phase, we are still investing in the mirroring effect where a partner will exhibit the qualities that we have ourselves—including emotional unavailability. So many times in working with numerous clients, I have to finally ask, "Yes, he is emotionally unavailable, and yes, the past few guys have been too—but instead of placing it all on them, are *you* emotionally unavailable?"

The answer always comes with excuses: They held back on being vulnerable because they had been hurt badly, or because they were afraid to show vulnerability, or even because they didn't know what it meant to be vulnerable. Yet the outcome is emotional unavailability, and so the same qualities they kept subconsciously seeking out were the very ones they were in possession of.

In some ways, we can look at them and say, Of course that would never be me. But when we are scared of finding out who we actually are, it's amazing how easily we let someone else fill in the blanks for us.

Our karmic love is different from our first love, but not so different that it will challenge us to step away from living our own bullshit. It can, however, make us better.

Early on in the karmic love, even though we're committed to doing it right, we become aware of a roller-coaster pattern in the relationship: when it's good, it's off the charts; but when it's bad, it seems nothing could get worse. And when we're low, the only thing we're focusing on is when and how we'll get to that next high.

These emotions, feelings, and experiences can range from whirlwind dates and trips to exotic places, to arguments that turn physical or therapist's visits after we've been cheated on for the umpteenth time.

THE LOVE BOMB

Very often, these relationships exhibit various personality tendencies or disorders—in ourselves, our partners, or both—including narcissism, codependency, and control or abuse of some kind. While not every karmic partnership includes one of these, it is a love that ultimately ends up hurting us more than actually helping us rise into better versions of ourselves.

In the beginning, such dysfunction will likely be minimal. It may even be masked by simple jealousy or insecurity, in which case we usually take it upon ourselves to try to fix our partner, and they us—not understanding that we're not really getting it right this time at all, but in fact setting off triggers that only send us deeper within ourselves and away from our partner.

Narcissists are very self-centered and manipulative. At first the narcissist will seem very sweet, attentive, and as if he just magically understands us. They may show us a great deal of attention whether it's texting, facetiming, or giving extravagant presents—they seem to want to make us the most important part of their world.

However, this is just how they hook their victims. This is the "love bombing" phase.

During the love bomb phase, we are their one and only. They take cues from us, learning how to more effectively manipulate our emotions. This emphasizes the mirroring effect, because not only are we falling in love with ourselves, they are also specifically projecting qualities they don't actually possess in order to engage us, attach us—and we end up falling fast and hard.

Love bombing comes like a whirlwind. The relationship develops very quickly. But what's really occurring is that narcissists want something from you. Perhaps it's the validation the relationship provides them, since they usually have very low self-confidence. But it can also be for material items or even their own source of identity because they see you in possession of some quality they desire.

Narcissists don't act alone, however—they need someone who is open to their attentions and game-playing behaviors. Ultimately, the perfect partner for the narcissist is the codependent, because the only thing she wants is to help validate her lover so that she can feel better about herself.

Karmic relationships can be controlling or abusive as well, because we've participated in a level of trauma bonding with them. Because of this, these relationships tend to be even more difficult to end than that with our soul mate.

Trauma bonding is loyalty to a destructive partner and partnership. We come together not because of an amazing healthy relationship, but because we both feel so miserable. This type of romantic connection is based on shared hurt, fears, and, yes, even karma. Trauma bonding is the belief that we can't do any better or we can't escape a particular cycle—even if we know we need to get out.

Relationships based on narcissism, codependency, abuse, or which are just simply unhealthy, coalesce around shared hurt or pain. They occur when we feel we don't deserve better, when we lack a positive self-image, worthiness, or are still learning to love ourselves.

The karmic relationship acts like a drug: We get high off of the good times, off the love bombing, the gifts, trips, and sex—so when we hit a rough spot, when we are disappointed or betrayed, have a huge blow-out fight, or even get cheated on . . . we stay. We stay because we're addicted to the positive feelings that we're using to supplement how we feel about ourselves. We aren't aware or don't know how to do our own self-work at this point, so we take the love drug from our karmic partner as a substitute.

The romantic choices we make from a position of healing will always be dramatically different from those made from wounding.

One of my clients, Maya, outwardly projected as having a high level of self-confidence. She radiated self-assurance, was very creative and ambitious—qualities that a narcissist is attracted to. She had no idea she had been participating in codependent, narcissist relationships for most of her life.

This cycle worked for some time. She had some great loves, helped a lot of men, but also got betrayed and suffered heartbreak numerous times—but she kept it up.

Under closer examination, you could see that she actually did not have a strong sense of self and used her codependent relationships with men to validate herself. One day, we began talking about worthiness and what healing meant to her, opening up the conversation about codependency. Sometimes awareness is like a light that suddenly goes on. I still remember the minute she saw her situation for what it was, saying in shock, "Oh my god, I'm not crazy, this actually is a real thing!" She was actually relieved that there was a reason behind the patterns in her relationships.

Maya began making changes immediately—but that also meant she was no longer the perfect victim for her beloved narcissist, and so the relationship had to end, along with her codependency cycles.

Once the relationship with our soul mate ends, we're looking for excitement, we're looking for fireworks and that feeling of being alive. We're wanting to feel like we've broken through the barriers set by our families and society, barriers that keep us from our best selves. So even though this new, karmic relationship is ultimately unhealthy, at the very least it's never boring, and it propels us into believing we're creating deeper levels of intimacy with our partner.

It's extremely common during this zero-to-sixty phase for

partners to commit or move in together very quickly because we feel like we've truly found ourselves in this other person; we feel like they complete us.

LETTING GO OF THE LACK

It's not uncommon to blatantly ignore issues in the beginning because the love feels so powerful. This is something that we're meant to experience because in truth this phase helps us understand that we can't look for another to make up for what we lack. We can't base how we feel about ourselves on how we are seen by another and, ultimately, we can't rely on anyone else to make us feel good about ourselves. If we keep using others to fill a void that we have within ourselves we will continue to go in and out of relationships.

We're determined to make this relationship work, to get it right; but we won't be able to because we haven't yet taken the time to get *us* right. We haven't taken the time to truly get right with who we are and the things that we have done and those done to us. We're still looking for external validation. It may not be through upholding the values that our families imposed upon us with our soul mate, but it's through the excitement and addictive nature of an unhealthy love that often ends up hurting us. Yet we don't think of actually walking away from it.

The fact that we need to get right with ourselves first before entering into a relationship isn't something that we're aware of at this phase of karmic love. We aren't thinking so much about being a specific type of person but rather how we can be a partner to this wild lover. We want to be able to give our partner certain things, to be seen a certain way, or even be needed by them on a financial or emotional level so that we feel important and needed ourselves.

We subconsciously believe that if we can get the relationship right, then we'll feel right too, not knowing that the course of this relationship isn't just destined to be a downfall but the kind of situation that ends in flames. We then have to make the choice to rise from the ashes.

What is interesting about both our soul mate and karmic love is that we do get glimpses of who we truly are during both relationships. We feel our intuition or emotional radar go off, but we lack the self-confidence to trust our feelings and so instead we focus on what is in front of us instead of what is within us.

In this case we are still focusing on the lack.

When we focus on the lack within relationships and within ourselves, then our only sources of validation and confidence are external. It's not about who we are, but about how someone else makes us feel; it's not about what we can do, but what we feel is possible if we're in relationship with this person. But it's also about us feeling like we aren't whole just because we're not in a romantic relationship.

To operate from lack is to still be connected to our ego because we haven't yet learned that everything we need, we already are; and everything we want, we already are in possession of. This not only includes self-confidence, esteem, and worthiness, but also love itself because the only reason we ever feel truly unloved is when we don't love ourselves.

We still are operating from ego, not only seeking those relationships that validate our unworthiness or superficially fuel our self-confidence but thinking that just because we want something to be right means that we will be able to make it right. Real forever love has very little to do with what we actually want. Instead, forever love is meant to occur, and is the ultimate purpose of the union.

Yet we can't give up control of our love life because we're still using it to define who we are and the place that we occupy within this world. So we hang on, we keep working, we ignore yet again the red flags that flash before our eyes and we hope that this time we won't be proven wrong.

THE FREE-WILL TANTRUM

"But I have free will" is a statement I hear echoed so many times from those defending why they do or don't do certain things. Really, it's the equivalent of a toddler tantrum.

Free will is the masquerade of ego in which we still think we can control everything, in which we still think we should or even can get our way or excuse our choices: "Yes, I know this relationship looks crazy from the outside but I have free will so I can choose it," or, "Yes, I am in love with that other person but I want to stay here in this relationship because I have free will."

At some point, though, we have to grow up and realize that it's not about ego, it's not about free will—it's about where that inner voice is telling us to go, what that voice is trying to tell us.

We could spend a lifetime using our free will yet never actually be happy.

In certain circumstances we even marry our karmic loves because we're so determined to not be wrong that we'll do anything to make it right—including using our free will. If we hadn't yet had children with our soul mate, then our karmic partner is the one that we will usually try marriage and family with. Often we meet these loves when we are younger, right after high school to late twenties, the time frame when we think we're doing things differently. Actually, all we are doing is following the plan set out for us, except we are doing it with someone who keeps us addicted through the ever-constant highs and lows of an unhealthy relationship.

What matters most during the honeymoon of our second love is simply making it work, without ever stopping to think if we should bother. It's the love that will send us to the counselor's or therapist's office within a year of being together because we're willing to try anything to get it right as long as it means we won't actually have to admit that it's already a lost cause. While relationship coaching is extremely beneficial if significant issues arise early in the relationship, especially related to the core values or beliefs of each person, it's also usually a sign that there are inherent differences within the connection that will make it very difficult to have a peaceful, healthy, long-term love.

Notice I didn't say they wouldn't be able to stay together, but only that the relationship wouldn't be maintained as a long-term, healthy love. This is because sometimes we opt for a free-will tantrum, and sometimes we don't make choices based on our hopes or well-being but rather on our fears and wounding.

For instance, I worked with Ashley, who had married and started a family with her karmic love. When she and I first met, she was several years into a marriage that had taken everything, including her peace of mind. She first approached me because she wanted my help to "make it right," even after her husband had cheated on her, transmitted an STD to her, neglected their children, and roughed her up. Even after one of their big fights, she was still trying to make it right, describing how amazing he was and how much she loved him.

Love bombing at its finest.

Sometimes we don't want to let go of something because we're afraid that it is our last chance at love or happiness, not actually knowing what would even fulfill that need of ours to begin with. So we decide not that we're unconditionally loved and accepted, not that this person helps us become a better version of ourselves, but rather that we are just afraid that if we let go we'll be alone forever.

This is the exact sentiment Ashley echoed to me during one of our first calls: "I can't be alone, I'm afraid if I leave him I'll end up alone forever and I've never actually been alone." I've heard that fear expressed by other women, so I told her the same thing I've told them: "The very thing we're most afraid of is the very thing we're meant to experience because until we do, we ultimately won't be free from these patterns."

This relationship is about becoming strong enough to stand on our own two feet.

STOP WAITING FOR PRINCE CHARMING AND RESCUE YOURSELF

Until we face our deepest fears, they will continue to hold power over us. In these situations we can become paralyzed with fear or even feel so stuck that we can't see a way out.

No healthy romantic partner will rescue you from the job of learning how to rescue yourself. It doesn't mean we're left entirely on our own fending for ourselves, but it does mean that we can't use one relationship to escape another.

Sometimes the heavy lifting has to be on us alone.

There is no way out of self-growth and there is no shortcut to it, either. At this phase, we're likely still ignoring all of the signs, we're trying to pretend that everything is fine—but deep down we know otherwise. It's not easy to get to this place of having to not only face our fears of being alone forever but also remove ourselves from a potentially unhealthy situation—but what we learn from this experience can never be taken away from us.

This love is about teaching us to be the hero of our own goddamn story.

It's up to us to pull ourselves out of the mud, to pull on our boss pants and handle our life—even if we have no idea how the hell we're going to do it. We need to change our patterns, to change who we attract, which means we need to change the vibration we're giving off.

Everything in life has a vibrational frequency. Emotions such as love and happiness hold a higher vibration, while jealousy, anger, and revenge hold a lower frequency. In order to actually start making better choices for ourselves, we need to stop trying to stick to a plan. I mean that we have to know when to bail, especially if the plane is already going down in flames.

No one needs to be a martyr for love.

In this stage maybe we're no longer trying to make our parents happy but we're still trying to not fail in love. As long as we're working more for a story line than a healthy relationship, then we'll continue to hold ourselves back and make lower vibrational choices.

It's about leveling up for ourselves.

Leveling up means raising our vibration by focusing on ourselves. We can then change the kind of people we attract. Once we start doing our own work, choosing ourselves over a story line, then our happiness—and consequently our vibration—inherently rises, and we begin to attract people on a similar level.

Love will never work out the way we think it should, mostly because the entire purpose of love is to learn and grow from the relationship, whether it lasts a month or until we draw our last breath on this earth. Love has the ability to transform us, to help us deal with our fears and wounding that we've been carrying around with us since childhood. It also has the ability to set us free from thinking that we can actually control whether or not a relationship ends.

Because in this phase, our karmic relationship, we will learn that we can't make something last that is supposed to end; we can't make something right that was never really meant to be. And ultimately we can't make any relationship work until we actually take the time to first succeed in the one that we have with ourselves.

So we love, we hurt, and we get hurt making our way through the early stage of this relationship, seeing the red flags but ignoring them, knowing that maybe this isn't the kind of love we've heard so much about but afraid to be wrong because that would mean we would be right back at the beginning.

Right back to being in the place where we were going to bed each evening alone and looking at no one else in the mirror but ourselves.

Yet this all happens as it's meant to: the cycle of relationships that we have to go through in order to make it to our third and final love. So maybe we spend years with our karmic partner, maybe we bounce back and forth between our safe soul mate and new loves, but ultimately we always work through relationship issues as we're meant to so that we can learn the necessary lessons once and for all.

Sometimes we don't want to see what is right in front of us, and sometimes what's right in front of us is precisely what we're meant to walk away from, but regardless, things can only change when how we see them begins to change. Which means that we have to give up trying to *make* something right.

Instead, let it be whatever it is meant to be, even if that turns out to be just one more lesson.

PART II

THE REALITY

We Bring Out the Worst in Each Other

They say the road to hell is paved with good intentions and there's no truer sentiment for this phase of our relationship journey. Yet we often like to place blame, we like to point fingers at our partner and make it seem like it's their fault that our relationship didn't work out, instead of actually realizing that just as it takes two to make love work—it also takes two for the relationship to crash and burn.

We start off our karmic love without realizing that we are projecting onto our lover the characteristics we think we want for ourselves: their wildness and freedom, their high-powered lives—whatever attracted us to them in the first place.

We try to be aware of differences, make different choices, and be more present, more accountable, more loving than we previously were, all with the expectation that if we change enough about how we operate within a relationship, we'll be able to have a better result. What we fail to realize, however, is that it's never about us doing something different on the outside, but rather about becoming something different on the inside that actually has the biggest effect on our relationships.

This stage of our karmic love is one of the most painful moments on the journey to finding real and lasting love, because we realize that we haven't come as far as we had hoped. We see just how wounded we still are and how much growing we still have to do—not just in terms of our intimate relationships, but also in our personal development. In order to truly learn our lessons and be able to take an honest look at ourselves and our motives, we need to be broken open to do so.

In the reality phase of our karmic love, we hurt each other, our fears surface, our old patterns come back out to play, and it's likely that we even believe that it's our soul mate we should have stayed with. After all, while the love may not have been as intense, it also never had the power to hurt us in the soul-wrenching way that our karmic love does.

We start to focus less on ourselves and what we did wrong, and become more obsessed with all the ways we were done wrong or can use to justify our own actions.

While we could have actually progressed on the journey of self-awareness since we first left our soul mate love, it's more likely that forward movement will become stagnant during this phase because we will feel an immense amount of guilt about once again not being able to make a relationship work or step up as our best selves. We fall back to the person that we were before, we blame the other person, we use others as a way to distract ourselves from dealing with the situation in front of us. In the process, not only are we *not* becoming our best selves, we become skilled in bringing out the worst in each other.

This is because we are set up in that addictive pattern of hurt and love bombing in order to shift the perspective from fixing ourselves to getting our next fix from the relationship.

Our karmic love is *supposed* to challenge us, to hurt us so profoundly that we have no other choice but to open up and look at the shit that we've spent so much time running from. It doesn't matter who we are or how much "work" we say that we've done on ourselves, the minute we feel our karmic love bombing cease and the reality creep in, we will automatically get triggered.

In the moment, this triggering can feel like betrayal.

It will feel like the worst possible thing to happen. But remember, the entire purpose of the relationship was to get to this point so that we could then be forced to grow and actually look at everything about ourselves that we've been trying to ignore.

WE CAN NEVER ESCAPE OURSELVES

Part of this journey in love is to learn that we can never escape our own self-work by throwing ourselves into a relationship. We can't mask our unhealed wounds or feelings of unworthiness because the triggers will keep resurfacing until we finally make the choice to deal with them.

Or because not dealing with them becomes impossible.

Self-work is never easy. It's also not a process that is truly ever over. We will progress and we will heal, but triggers will always exist. We are humans after all. None of us is safe from the realities of life and love.

To be in a healthy relationship is not to never experience hard times, arguments, or even triggers, but to be able to process them without projecting or blaming. It's the difference between "Look what you did to me!" and "I feel this way because . . ." Our emotional maturity expands, along with our ability to recognize an emotion, a feeling, without actually setting up shop and existing within it.

There is no perfect relationship.

It doesn't matter if it's our first love, second, or even our twin flame. A good relationship will in fact force us to grow, to look at things differently, and to work through those feelings that are holding us back, not only from being our best selves but from being in the type of relationship that we hope for.

Realizing that we can't escape ourselves and our self-work means that our perspective shifts from an outward focus to an internal one. It becomes less about what the other person is doing and more about why we feel a particular way.

Part of this process is ceasing to take things personally. If our partner is having a bad day and is moody or grumpy, we no longer assume that we are the reason why. If that great guy we've been dating takes a couple days to respond to a text, we're not thinking, *Oh, he must not like me, I can't believe I said what I did, I must have sounded so dumb to him.*

When we start to understand that each person is having their own individual experience and is writing their own story in this life, apart from us, then we can understand that nothing anyone does is because of us. We begin to understand our ego and learn to not operate from the thoughts and beliefs that it holds. Ego thinks everything is about her, ego thinks that the reason people return our calls or ghost us is about her: that essentially we have control over how another person behaves and the choices they make.

As we grow through our self-work, we come to understand that we have our story and our partner has theirs. Once we learn how to not take something personally, then we open up an entirely new way of relating to each other.

Hailey was married and admittedly within the narcissist/codependent cycle for the majority of her adult life when she and I first began working together. She had divorced this man several years ago yet was still struggling with how to relate to her new partner. In her new relationship, she found herself triggered all the time, getting upset if he didn't text her back right away or delayed making plans—really, anything that reminded her of the dynamic of her karmic love.

We spoke in great detail about how it was positive that her new partner was triggering her because it meant she got to look at what was happening and react differently. It was an opportunity to learn that not every man is her ex, and that in this relationship, she had to approach her new partner completely differently. She was learning to express her feelings from the start instead of being passive-aggressive; when she needed something, she was learning to speak up instead of becoming angry because he didn't instinctively know.

And most of all, she was learning that he had his own life. He was starting a business, dealing with family, and sometimes did just want to hang out with his friends. Instead of taking every little bump personally—"He's going to break up with me" or "He must not really like me"—she was learning to change her inner dialogue.

Learning to be in a relationship in the wake of our karmic love is also the process of self-work because we have to raise our level of awareness when it comes to our triggers and reactions.

But in order to be able to get to this space of approaching relationships in a healthy way, we first have to be able to name *why* we feel certain ways about what our partner may or may not do. It means that we first have to be able to admit that whatever is going wrong in the relationship isn't just our partners' fault, both past and present, but that we have a part in it too.

Often at this stage, we start name-calling and reducing our partner to nothing more than a cliché, sending our best friends memes about how you don't know what you have until it's gone, or you'll always regret losing a good woman.

While these feelings are valid, they don't actually take the place of the self-work that is the purpose of this stage. We have to be open to what behaviors or feelings were present during the relationship that led both partners to the current situation, which may now feel like a toxic love.

IT TAKES TWO TO BE TOXIC

Often in our karmic love, we project all the negativity onto our partner and paint them as an asshole, a fuckboy, or maybe just emotionally unavailable, without actually taking responsibility for our part in the dynamic.

Even if we are honest, loving, faithful, and sweet, and doing nothing "wrong," the truth is that we still chose this relationship and allow the ongoing behaviors. Are we the ones cheating or lying? No, but that doesn't mean that we're free from being responsible for having chosen this type of relationship.

When we are in relationships, what we see is only a reflection of where we are at the time; and so within toxic relationships, we are ultimately being presented with a part of ourselves that we haven't yet healed. After all, there is always a reason the nice girl dates the bad boy, even if we're not ready to acknowledge it.

This means that in order to no longer attract a toxic relationship, we need to address ourselves.

A toxic love is defined by its unhealthiness—for our minds, bodies, and souls. But we need to go deeper and actually name these behaviors so that we can get to the root of what is going on within the karmic connection. What I've come to realize is that the definition of a healthy relationship differs from person to person. When I'm working with a new client and they say that they want a healthy relationship, I always ask them to keep a journal about what that means to them. While perhaps the structure is similar from one person's journal to another, the details often differ. It is in the details that we come to a deeper understanding of what our core needs are.

While we are first presented with our core needs in our soul mate relationship, it takes moving through and processing both our first and second loves to get to a place where we know what those core needs authentically are—but more: where we're able to *advocate* for our needs as well.

As previously mentioned, our core needs first surface in our soul mate love. Here, we begin to understand that just because a relationship can check certain boxes and make others satisfied with our life choices, it doesn't necessarily mean that our needs are truly fulfilled. Yet we entered into this new karmic relationship believing it will be different without doing the work to truly understand our love motive.

It's always easier to think another partner is going to fix us rather than take the time to do it for ourselves.

THE FIVE FOUNDATIONS

When I first asked my client Sam about what a healthy relationship meant to her, she stated that she needed quality time and transparency, meaning that whatever man she was with wouldn't be texting other women behind her back. Nina said that it was important to her to communicate a lot within a relationship and to feel that the man she was with was putting in effort.

While these are valid feelings, they reflect core needs more than just the overall definition of a healthy relationship.

A healthy relationship needs to have several factors in order to be able to function in a way that best serves both individual partners. When I'm working with clients, I compare building a relationship to building a house. While everyone's all excited to paint and decorate a finished house, no one actually wants to go and build the foundation and the basement. As in building a house, the basement represents the foundation of a relationship, the part that is respon-

sible for holding up that house that we love so much. If the foundation of a home is shoddy, cracked, or not aligned, then the house will
fall—and the same is true for any relationship.

I have developed what I call the Five Foundations—a collection
of tools you can use to build that strong foundation, just like we'd
need for a home. I suggest implementing them during the interview
phase of a new relationship. They are: communication, honesty, accountability, respect, and forgiveness.

During the interview phase, we are just beginning to know each
other, a period when we as women often give away all our power and
think "Oh will he like me?" or "Will he want to go out with me
again?" instead of stopping and thinking about whether this human
is even someone we want in our life as a friend, let alone as a lover.

Communication

The first component of the Five Foundations is communication.
This doesn't just mean being in touch throughout the day or even
texting if you're going to be home late. Communication, rather,
needs to be the driving force behind any relationship. Many men
balk when they hear "communication" because they think it means
that we'll want to talk for hours every single day about our feelings.
In truth, it's a way of life that can dramatically affect all of our
relationships.

Communication means that we are committing to talking things
through. It means we're going to try our best to not shut down, and
to discuss triggers, feelings, or different situations as they arise. It

means we are going to be open and forthcoming about where we are within the relationship, whether or not our core needs are being met, or if we are just plain scared. It means that we share our dreams with our partners, not just what we had for lunch. To commit to putting communication first means that if problems arise, we're not going to leave, we're going to stay and talk through it, no matter how difficult that may be.

For me, I need space within a relationship—but I also need physical touch and a lot of cuddling! Rather than getting upset with my partner because they constantly text or call, I voice that to them, saying, "In order to be my best self I need to have quiet time to process my day," and so when it comes up, they already know and there are no surprises.

The same is true of my need for physical touch. Rather than sit on the other end of the couch giving the evil eye because the man in my life hasn't put his arm around me, I'll snuggle up to him or ask for him to put his arm around me. I'll let him know that I need that physical touch because it's an important part of feeling connected to him.

This brings me to the most important part of communication—preemptive communication.

This seems to be the aspect that we all struggle with at one time or another. This is because if it's not viewed from a place of healing, it can come to feel like a lack of freedom or trust, when in reality it's the single most important form of communication. When couples can put this type of communication in place, it cuts down dramatically on misunderstandings and arguments, which of course leaves more time for the happy, in-love moments.

In preemptive communication with our partner, we actually bring something up and talk about it before it becomes an issue. It would sound something like "My old girlfriend texted me yesterday" or "I'm feeling like this is going too fast and I need some time before we move in together." It's bringing up an issue or telling our partners about a problem prior to it actually becoming that drop-down argument that we can't get back from. We can't ultimately practice this type of communication with our partners, however, until we can also be honest and not judge ourselves for feeling or thinking a certain way. We must also leave behind any assumptions about how we think the other person might react.

It sounds basic, but if we can actually tell our partner ahead of time that we're feeling triggered, or scared, or that there's a chance our old boyfriend might be at the reunion next weekend, then we usually can avoid the argument altogether. But to do this we need honesty—both with ourselves and with the person we're in a relationship with.

Which is the second point.

Communication is not just for those times when we spoke with an ex but for our needs as well, because when we can be an advocate for our own needs, as space and touch are for me, then we will be building a more transparent and understanding connection with our partner.

Neither of us will expect the other to read our minds. And we won't have to, because we're going to actually be talking about what matters.

Honesty

Many times when we think of being honest, we mean that we're simply not going to lie. In fact, it's so much more than that.

Honesty is defined as being free from deceit and untruthfulness, as being sincere. We often think of this in terms of what we expect to give to or receive from a lover, friends, or family. Yet we also struggle with being honest with ourselves—about who we are, and what we want from love and life in general. It requires us to be our true selves and not try to squeeze into any roles or play the parts that others may want us to.

When we are honest with ourselves, we own who we are—scars, blemishes, warts, and all. We don't make excuses or downplay what we want or think. Only then can we also communicate that honesty to others.

Lena always had an internal battle because what she wanted from a relationship was different from what society seems to tell us we are supposed to want. She was open to love, she was ready to commit to a partner, but she wanted to do it in a way that felt right for her. Through her own experiences, Lena came to learn that she never wanted to live full-time with someone. She loved the idea of sleepovers, even giving him a drawer or two at her place. But she knew that she needed at least a few nights to herself each week to read, meditate, or just do nothing.

In many societies across the world, people like Lena are made to feel beyond the pale because that is not the norm that we tradition-ally abide by. It was, however, *her* truth.

While she was comfortable expressing her wants and needs in our discussions about it, Lena was hesitant to get into a relationship because she dreaded having to explain her point of view about per-sonal space. Eventually she met Clint, a musician who traveled often for work, and suddenly that big problem of speaking her truth wasn't a big deal at all.

Once she got comfortable with expressing her truth, the universe responded to her vibration as well and connected her with Clint, someone who could satisfy a core need of hers.

When we're honest with ourselves, we can start speaking our truth—not just the truth about what our goals in life or within a relationship are, but also how we really feel about that vacation spot, or that elopement locale. If we start withholding truth from ourselves, it translates to our relationships, and that is when com-munication starts to break down, creating conflict within the relationship.

If we do not know our truth, then we will not be able to express it to another. And that means we'll be less likely to actually live an authentic life—or relationship.

Accountability

To be accountable within a relationship means that before we worry about being faithful to a partner, we first are going to learn how to be faithful to ourselves, our dreams, and our needs. When we can practice accountability, we can then also practice honesty. When we are accountable, we have and are aware of our own personal set of morals and limits that we hold ourselves to.

This is something we have to do for ourselves. It has to come from within. No one, not even that amazing great love, can do it for us or force us to be better than we are.

When we hold ourselves accountable, we are responsible, not just in the literal sense of getting to work or paying bills on time, but more so to our souls, our hearts, and that inner essence of who we are. To be accountable to ourselves means we're not going to sell out if someone doesn't like the partner that we choose; it means that we're not going to stay in that life-draining job just because the pay is good; and it doesn't mean we're going to unconditionally sacrifice our integrity—in other words, lie—to protect another's feelings.

There is no room for self-sacrifice in healthy relationships. Without accountability, both to self and to our partner, then there is no way that we can build foundations solid enough to make it through the worst of times.

A few years back, Taylor contacted me because she didn't know what to do about her relationship. She felt she knew who she was or at least was working toward it, she had good communication with her partner, Kyle, and they loved each other. But she had doubts about where to take the relationship because neither her family nor friends were very supportive—not because Kyle wasn't a good partner, but because they felt he didn't look the part: he was from a different racial and socioeconomic background. While none of that mattered to Taylor, the stress of the situation was taking its toll.

During our conversations, we talked about accountability, and how it helps strengthen autonomy as we grow.

Autonomy is defined as being able to make choices and decisions in our own best interest, to be confident in the choices we make, and not be coerced or influenced by others. In many ways, our search for autonomy means that we will likely have to rebel against parental figures at some point in order to gain mental and emotional maturity.

But in romantic relationships, autonomy gets a bit more complicated.

We love our family and we love our partner. It should be that simple. Taylor began to understand, however, that the more confidently she claimed her partner and her partnership, the more her family would at least begin to respect the relationship, even if they never fully accepted it. No one else is going to live our life, not even our moms or sisters. Therefore, we must claim accountability—gladly—for our most important decisions: who we love, what work we do, whether to have children, or not.

Respect

I hear many clients speaking of respect without actually defining what this word means to them; and of course, as with any aspect of love, it first has to begin with ourselves. Respect is the admiration and positive feelings that we have for someone; because of that, we treat them with loyalty, patience, faithfulness, and understanding. This means that in respecting ourselves, we extend those same qualities to our own thoughts, feelings, and behaviors.

When we fully respect ourselves, how we carry and think of ourselves changes: We don't beat ourselves up over choices or supposed failures. We know we're trying our best and that one bad day doesn't mean we're a bad person.

Within a relationship, we extend to our partner the respect we already have given ourselves. Through respect, we are accountable for our feelings and actions, and we communicate honestly, all without feeling like we're sacrificing our freedom or our ability to live life in the way that we want.

It means that before we view our partner as a lover, we look at them as a person whom we admire, someone we see, and feel pride, love, and gratitude that we get to share our life with them. When we are honest with, accountable to, and respectful of our partner, it won't be a chore to be upfront if we're unsure about meeting their parents at the holidays. It means not worrying there will be a fight if we tell them that our ex texted us last week. In short, we are not living with a time bomb waiting to go off, but rather with someone whom we love and admire, and who loves and admires us and our qualities as well.

Respecting our partner means that we see them as an individual first, a lover second.

Forgiveness

Look at the word *forgiveness*: "for" + "give." It means that we're extending, giving something, to another—but also to ourselves. And so forgiveness is never earned, it's never proven, it's never a matter of being deserved, it's literally just meant to be given.

As humans, we mess up. We don't always do our best, we do those things sometimes that we know we shouldn't, and sometimes we just doubt ourselves, and so we make mistakes, we fuck up.

Sometimes even with that great love, but what can always bring us back to ourselves and our relationship is unconditional forgiveness. This isn't about just saying "I'm sorry" or "I forgive you" but rather is the desire to try, to do our best, to apologize, to make our wrong right, and to show that while we may not be perfect, we're committed to doing better than we did yesterday.

When we have that desire to make forgiveness an action, then everything else becomes doable.

It means that we know we have work to do, it means that we know we're still learning, healing, and trying to learn who we are. When we act to forgive, it means we're not giving up. We're not taking the easy way out; we're in it, whether that means posting our Man Crush photos because we're feeling so in love, or screaming and yelling as tears roll down our face.

Not one of us is perfect. We have all had those moments where we weren't our best selves. Whether we were hurting ourselves or trying to escape pain, we've all been at our worst at one point or another.

Think of your worst possible moment. I'm talking about secret to the grave, maybe only your best friend knows—maybe even worse. The moment in your life that you would never want anyone to know about. Now think about that being the standard by which you are judged.

This is what happens when we don't truly forgive someone. We end up holding their worst moments against them. We withhold forgiveness because that moment was too awful, too hurtful, or because we want them to suffer.

But if we don't want our worst moment held against us, then we can't hold another to theirs.

We forgive because that is the only way to continue to build our foundation within a relationship. Maybe there are betrayals that end a connection altogether, but even in those moments, forgiveness isn't only possible, it's required.

Navaeh felt she continually practiced forgiveness. She was incredibly spiritual, she tried to help others and live life as best she could. Together she and her partner, Marcus, felt like the world was a better place when they were together, stopping to talk to the homeless, finding ways to bring light to people's lives, and generally just trying to spread the love as much as they could.

So when Marcus suddenly ghosted her and looked like he was pursuing another woman, Navaeh didn't know what to do. She was angry, hurt, and confused that somehow this person who seemed to share a part of her soul could turn around and hurt her in this way.

One of the things she and I first spoke about is that anger is not a primary emotion.

Anger is only the result of another feeling: hurt, disappointment, frustration at things not going the way we wanted, or even fear. So we took apart her anger: she felt abandoned and betrayed by Marcus. Once her feelings were broken down in this way, they were more easily addressed. We talked about where those feelings of abandonment and betrayal stemmed from in her life and how we could use this current pain to heal something she hadn't even been aware of.

We also looked at his actions, which were hurtful. Remember hurt people hurt people? Navaeh came to understand that because Marcus was still hurting from wounds that hadn't yet healed, he then hurt her. It didn't make it okay, but it did allow her to understand and forgive him. And to accept that this had occurred and that ultimately perhaps it was necessary because it allowed for greater healing for both of them.

They are still in progress together, working on themselves, their connection to each other, and still very much in love. None of that would have been the case, however, had Navaeh not been able to forgive him.

BREAKING OUR OWN HEARTS

While love can mean many things, the single defining factor is never giving up. This can be why our karmic love breaks our heart.

We wanted this love to last, we felt that we had given them more of who we are than anyone before. We loved deeper and shared more. We sacrificed our best self because the relationship shook us to our core. Still, not only are we falling apart, we aren't even the people we thought we were. Suddenly he's not returning our texts for days and giving us the silent treatment, while we stalk social media trying to guess who has his attention now.

What we have to realize is that this phase of karmic love will challenge us: Are we holding ourselves accountable to our own personal standards? Are we respecting ourselves, being honest with ourselves? In most cases, karmic passion brings us to this sorry state because we aren't.

But that is the point of all of this.

There is no way to actually become better until we hit bottom, until we realize that whatever we were doing is no longer working. Quite honestly, until we get sick of our own shit, we're going to keep trying to get by without really having to do that soul-wrenching, sick-to-your-stomach self-work. Think of Jake Gyllenhaal and Anne Hathaway in the 2010 film *Love and Other Drugs*; Jake's character, Jamie, is a very happy playboy who simply enjoys women and the next conquest. He's not thinking about self-work, about intimacy, or even what feelings he might have stumbled into. Meanwhile, Anne's character, Maggie, is a woman with Parkinson's who has made it her full-time job to not get attached to people or let them too far within her walls.

They operated without much honesty, respect, or accountability, even to themselves. But they were comfortable, and so in the beginning of the relationship, they had a great time: tons of easy sex and fun. Neither had any intention of falling in love, and certainly neither wanted to get sucked into dreaded commitment. So when both realized that they had already fallen, they resorted to sabotage and self-destruction. They broke up, they tried to be with other people, but deep down they missed each other and the connection they felt.

That was when the hard work began. They both began to recognize their new-found desires and needs. Only once that was complete were they able to actually be there for each other.

Our karmic love breaks us so that we are open enough to do our own work and let in our third love. Even though we had every intention of being better, of staying faithful, vulnerable, or even just honest, the reality is that we couldn't do that for another because during this phase we hadn't yet learned to do that fully for ourselves.

We can only extend to another what we have first learned to do for ourselves. If we're still struggling to accept or respect ourselves, then we won't truly be able to offer that to another because our hands and our heart will be empty.

We love others in the same manner that we love ourselves.

HEALING OURSELVES

The love bombing kept us hooked. Otherwise, there's no way we would have stuck around for the lessons that this love has to teach us. In the beginning, the love bombing provided a great distraction. We didn't have to think about the hard stuff, and at times it was even wonderful to have someone to project all of our insecurities upon so we could feel better.

But there comes a time when we've finally had enough of that roller-coaster ride between love bombing and pain.

This is the point when our karmic love comes along and rips the Band-Aid off our emotional wounds and triggers with no warning, no explanation. They just sit there pointing to it and saying, "You know you're bleeding, right?"

At this point, we see that the person we thought was our be-all and end-all is not going to make any effort to cover our hurt or to help us. Of course, that is our job and no one else's, but we become angry. We want someone else to do the hard work! We become confused, bitter, and even resentful that this person who tore off the Band-Aid and ripped off the illusion that everything is just fine isn't going to do anything to actually make us feel better or help us heal.

This is exactly the realization we need to come to and the purpose of this kind of relationship. In fact, both partners are usually bleeding and even rubbing salt in the wounds. You will hear things like, "Oh, you're insecure because you were cheated on before— okay, now I'll start liking every picture this chick posts on Instagram." Or, "You were abandoned as a child by your dad—okay, then I'm going to keep leaving you and giving you the silent treatment too."

It's gut-wrenching, and honestly, it makes many of us feel like we're going crazy because we don't understand how this connection that felt so cosmically designed in the beginning could now leave us bleeding more profusely than ever before.

The sad thing about this relationship is that it can occur again. And again. And again. While for the most part, we have three great, meaningful, and poignant loves in our lives, they also serve as the three archetypes of relationships or lovers that we will experience in a lifetime, because we don't always learn the necessary lessons the first time around.

We can experience multiple karmic partners, not because that one great forever love isn't out there, but because no matter how many times we say we're ready for a healthy relationship, until we actually change our behavior—not his, ours—it will just be déjà vu all over again.

With our karmic love, it's common for us to have as many as it takes until we learn the hard lessons that we are meant to. One client, Laurie, only dated men who were emotionally unavailable, lived with their mothers, and didn't have a stable job. His name changed multiple times, as did the specifics, but she repeated the same pattern, not seeing until the third time around that she was stuck in a self-destructive but comfortable routine because that way, it was always his fault and she never had to be accountable for her own actions.

Once she recognized the pattern, she saw that her codependency and fear of intimacy were actually attracting a particular kind of man. She saw that her addiction came in the form of the validation she received by helping them financially. Meanwhile, she was safe from any emotional attachment because they would never be able to offer her the type of emotional depth she craved yet was scared of at the same time.

She attracted exactly what she needed, emotionally, until she was finally able to face it.

WE HAVE TO FEEL IT TO HEAL IT

As long as we remain unhealed from the wounds we first started off with, we're just going to keep bleeding on partners who never actually were the cause of that original pain. They didn't abandon us as children, they didn't make us feel invalidated or worthless as teens, they didn't make us question ourselves, and they didn't even lie to us. All that baggage was what we ourselves brought to the relationship. These are *our* wounds, and because we haven't yet healed them, we bled all over our soul mate (though they probably bled all over us, too). We bled all over our karmic partner—and probably more than one partner—because we didn't take responsibility for our own healing.

We think that every time we fall in love, the purpose of it is to make us feel good, forever. Otherwise, who among us would sign up if we could already see the expiration date?

See that cute guy playing pool, the bartender across the room, and the one in the green shirt laughing with friends? What would we do if we knew ahead of time that one would be a one-night stand, one might last six months, and maybe the third would last three years and end with a broken engagement? Which would you choose?

Would it make a difference if you knew from the beginning that this love's purpose in your life was for it to actually expire, so that you could move on to do the real work—to heal yourself?

Our karmic love is never supposed to last, no matter how many we have, no matter how long we're together or if we even marry and have children. There's too much left undone here. Its sole purpose is to be that mirror so that we can no longer ignore our own issues. This love comes into our lives and hurts us so deeply so that we stop projecting and blaming, and start being accountable for ourselves, our actions, and specifically our wounds. So that we can finally heal and stop bleeding on those who weren't part of our original pain.

This love is about having no choice but to face our feelings, even those that we have buried possibly since childhood. Yes, going back to childhood is sometimes seen as a cliché, but as a good friend of mine once said, "Clichés are true for a reason." We learn the rules of life in childhood, whether that means trusting our intuition or not letting anyone get too close so we don't get hurt.

What we absorb as children becomes part of our blueprint as adults.

There are wonderful things that we learned and had instilled in us as children. There are also others we can look at as opportunities for us to grow. What we come to see during this love phase, though, is that nothing will actually be right on the outside until we get ourselves right on the inside.

PART III

THE LESSON

Sometimes Love Isn't Meant to Last

The hardest breakup to have is the one that we know needs to happen but that we don't want to occur. For many of us, there comes a point when we have finally admitted to ourselves that our karmic love relationship is no longer healthy, or perhaps it never was. We are finally aware that the relationship doesn't feel good to our soul, that it doesn't honor who we are, and in many ways, we've had to swallow down our truth to even stay with this person for as long as we did. But none of this changes the fact that sometimes the relationship ends before the love does.

A relationship lasting and love lasting are two very different things.

Often we are able to admit to ourselves the relationship is over only when we've hit rock bottom. Maybe we discover we're being cheated on, lied to, or realize that who they pretended to be with us wasn't who they truly were. The only thing that hitting bottom does, though, is make us aware that we must do something, not that we no longer love that person.

For those not in their karmic love or those who have managed to escape a relationship like this so far, it seems so easy: "just dump them," "block their number," or "go out and date someone else" are just a few of the sentiments that our well-intentioned friends say to us in an effort to help us move on. Unfortunately, it's impossible to just "get over" our karmic love, because the only way through to an ending is our own growth and healing.

Just because we are aware someone isn't good for us doesn't mean that the very next day we will box up our feelings and address them "Return to Sender."

ONCE WE'VE LEARNED THE LESSON, WE NO LONGER NEED THE TEACHER

Realizing that this relationship isn't healthy is only the first step in moving on from this love. It's only the first step to understanding the lessons so that we don't repeat similar patterns or cycles; and it's only the beginning of getting to where we are truly ready for our forever love. At least, remember, karmic love is the final lesson we have to absorb before finding that forever love, that healthy, amazing "let's fall asleep under the stars" kind of love.

Moving on from our karmic love means being vulnerable and accountable, not just with another person but with ourselves.

Once we begin to see the reality of our karmic love, the first thing we tend to do is try to figure out how to fix the situation or our partner. Now, as you read this, you may say to yourself, "Of course we can't solely fix a relationship and we sure as hell can't fix another person," but part of this process is actually trying to get past being afraid or unwilling to move on. Sometimes we even tell ourselves that it's easier to stay and figure out how to make things work than it would be to start over with someone new, as if unhappiness is something that we should become accustomed to.

But our "teachers" also may panic when this relationship starts to spiral downward. Just as we have built our identity on being in a toxic relationship or misunderstood, they have built theirs around it as well. They may feel afraid that they are losing control, that they aren't needed anymore, or any number of losses they anticipate as the relationship begins to come apart.

While we know that there are unhealthy traits present in the connection, this fear of future losses will often trigger our partners into becoming more possessive or controlling. They may become more jealous and arguments may escalate as they feel us growing away from them.

Brianna agonized for some time in this phase of her relationship, becoming increasingly afraid of her partner, Austin. He had always been controlling and had exhibited some narcissistic tendencies, but once Brianna and I started working together, this behavior began to escalate.

Together we began looking at his behavior, her role within the relationship, and why she subconsciously sought out an experience like this one. As she got stronger and started to look for another place to live, Austin became very paranoid and jealous, thinking she was with another man. At first Brianna wanted to fix him, even if she didn't want to be with him anymore.

But finally I had to tell her: "Your relationship is the plane and it's going down! Put your oxygen mask on before anyone else's—including Austin's." It was a hard thing for her to do, but finally she realized that it was the only way to end this cycle. She ended up moving back to her family home and cutting all communication with Austin.

It seems ridiculous that we need to experience these kinds of extremes in order to learn that not only can we never fix anyone, but that we have to prioritize our own healing. Nonetheless, it is all worth it if we actually do learn the lesson.

We can't force someone to be their best self or even take responsibility for their actions. We can't prove to someone that we deserve better, and we can't be so loving and kind that someone will want to stop sleeping around or playing the field. We can't do anything in order for someone else to "get it," for them to see us as we see ourselves and begin to give us what any loving partner deserves in a relationship.

The first step in understanding what we *do* deserve can only be taken once we admit that we're not currently receiving it. During the reality phase of this love, we start to see the truth of what was going on, and begin to see more clearly what the qualities of a healthy relationship are. Consciously or unconsciously, we begin to assert our own needs. We begin to practice self-love.

One of the primary purposes of this love isn't only to shift our focus on love as the be-all and end-all of our life, but also to challenge us to begin the practice of self-love. The reason that these are so closely tied is that until we get to that place where we do actually have love for ourselves and can live as if we do, we won't be able to actually walk away and leave our karmic love.

A TIME-OUT FROM LOVE

There was a period in my life when I knew that I would be no good to anyone. I knew that honestly I was a flippin' hot mess and a disaster just waiting to happen. My heart had been broken too many times and I knew I was looking to the men in my life to give me the validation that I couldn't give myself.

So I decided to put myself in a love time-out.

I decided to be single, to be abstinent, and to work on me. I had a goal of one year without any sex, and I know what you're thinking and, yes, it was hard—but it was also really worth it. It taught me a lot about myself, about what I used men for, and really why I was constantly looking to men to make choices for me when I was actually more than capable of being the boss of my own life.

It was during this time I realized that even though I was more than capable—I wasn't willing.

I still had so much self-doubt, and rather than worrying about my own life or where to go from here, I was concerned about who wanted me or not, or if I would be single forever. Yes, it's normal, but I had gotten fed up with my normal and really tired of defining myself based on my relationship status.

So I decided no dating, no sex, and no men for one year.

That year was my chance to get me right, to not distract myself with OkCupid or Tinder; to not be looking for Mr. Right every time I went out with my friends and instead to just sit back and actually give myself a chance to deal with myself. It was a deep process, one that wasn't always comfortable. There were many times I held myself as I fell asleep telling myself that I was worthy, I was loved, because I missed that external validation; I missed the comfort that the touch of a man could provide.

What I hadn't realized, though, was that in those moments I was actually telling myself that I loved *me*.

I wasn't just taking time to get myself right so I could have a better relationship with a partner. I was doing it to find what made me tick and, honestly, to fall in love with myself.

In love, there is no right or wrong. We are meant to have failed relationships, we are meant to break hearts and have ours broken, we're meant to experience unhealthy relationships—so that we can continue to grow and become better through the lessons we learn about ourselves.

But sometimes our karmic love becomes the father of our children, and leaving him behind isn't easy.

WE CAN'T ESCAPE OUR KARMA

Our karmic relationships are addictive, and while the love bombing is a big part of that—so is the sex.

This means that not only do we sometimes marry our karmic love, but we also tend to have hookups more often too. Because we tend to not meet our third love until later in life, we usually will have a first marriage and/or children with our soul mate or karmic love.

While coparenting with our soul mate can eventually be a wonderful experience, that is not true for our karmic love.

If children are involved, we do not have an easy out from our karmic love. These situations can be incredibly difficult, and ultimately can make us feel like we're stuck with our karmic love even if we ended things long ago.

But if we look for the lessons in these tough situations, if we can figure out what our soul was meant to learn, then we can actually end up improving our parenting relationship.

Kiara married her karmic love—the cycle of the love bombing was just too much to resist. But about five years into it, she knew that she had to get out. Not only were they married, but they had had a child together as well. She knew that even if she were to leave, she would never actually be free of this man.

She and I met a few years after her divorce. She was upset because this man could still push her buttons, just as he had when they were married. So we talked about her triggers; how he played off them and what role she played in allowing the behavior and participating in the cycle.

For Kiara, it came down to boundaries.

She was always the nice one and never wanted to hurt anyone's feelings, which meant even once she had decided to leave her ex, she still tried to be his friend. She still thought that she could make things better and that he might improve his behavior once the marriage was over. No surprise to learn that this never happened!

Instead, Kiara and I worked on instilling boundaries with her ex, which meant at this point she was not his friend. She was a mother first and she set down parameters of what felt good for her. Of course, her ex balked at these, but after a few months he gradually realized his tactics could no longer push her buttons and so he had to resort to different behavior as well.

This meant that this cycle with her karmic love, the father of her child, had not only come to a close because they cleared their karma—but that they both had learned a lesson from it.

THE IMPOSTER

One of the problems in identifying our karmic love is that we can mistake it for our twin flame. This is known as the "false twin flame" phenomenon. This is the one that we wish was right, the one where the love feels so unbelievably deep, we can't stay away. We tell ourselves this is The One instead of seeing the reality—addiction to the love bomb.

This is just one more lesson we're meant to learn before clearing our karma and being in a place to receive healthy love.

False twin flame is a term used to describe a relationship and connection that feels as strong as the real thing, that it is destiny, and irreplaceable. With true twin flames, while there may be some of the same karmic passion in the beginning, there will never be unhealthy behaviors such as codependency and narcissism. It will never translate to a decade of being the other woman or being cheated on simply because the twin flame is about a connection that is *only* possible once all other karma has been cleared.

I remember being blown away by my karmic love, and in the beginning, I thought he was my twin flame. I remember remarking that it felt like the earth moved the first time I stood on tiptoes and his lips touched mine. Never before had I had that same chemistry or attraction, so I interpreted that as meaning we had a deep spiritual connection of two souls instead of seeing the reality of the situation, instead of seeing it for what it was: that we were placed in each other's life to learn and to clear the karma that we had accumulated in past lives.

For me, the karma that was involved—the lesson I learned—was to realize my personal worth, and to never love another more than I love myself. I absolutely had some codependent behaviors and enjoyed feeling needed in my romantic relationship, often to the detriment of my partner. Even though I knew what I deserved from a partner, I constantly made excuses as to why I didn't receive it, in part because I was afraid to lose the karmic high the relationship brought, but also because I was afraid that I would never feel like that again.

I hadn't ever had to walk away from someone while still loving them, hadn't been faced with the decision that I could either practice compassion and love toward them or myself—but not both.

This dilemma is common in the karmic love cycle because we get so used to putting the other person before ourselves, not just because of the strength of the connection, but also because we're trying to fix them at the expense of ourselves. No healthy relationship should ever make us sacrifice who we are. No healthy relationship should have us compromise our worth or what we feel we deserve—and I'm not speaking of jewels or helicopter dates, but of decency, respect, and trust. And, especially, no relationship should ever make us put aside self-love in order to be able to love our partner.

Another term I've recently begun using with clients to describe this karmic love/false twin flame is our *catalyst love* because without this person, we wouldn't be on this new path. We wouldn't be able to look at ourselves differently, to explore different aspects of life and consciousness, and we wouldn't be in the place where we could advocate for ourselves in a healthy relationship.

We all want to find our twin flame—but we have to learn that to get there, we have to clear a lot of karma, which potentially could be from having experienced lifetimes with this particular partner, hurting each other over and over again.

Sydney came to me wanting help in cutting the ties between herself and the man she believed was her twin flame. She had spoken to numerous intuitives and healers and knew that the two of them had experienced many lifetimes together.

When we first met, I told her that there is no cutting ties of any kind with any type of love—the tie itself disappears when our lesson is learned and they are no longer needed.

While we worked together, this man came in and out of her life, never offering to meet her needs or make her a priority—she still believed this man was her twin flame even though he treated her like dirt. He slept with other women, ghosted her, was emotionally unavailable, and overall lacked any integrity or honesty in his behavior toward her. But Sydney held on because she couldn't see him any other way until she finally had no choice. She called it quits—but in truth there was nothing to really call quits, except her having hope that this man, who was so very unhealthy for her, would one day be able to love her in the ways that she needed.

In time, she became stronger, she healed, and she cleared the karma and hurt they had accumulated through various lifetimes together. It's because of this man that Sydney embarked on a spiritual journey—not just to grow and heal herself, but to discover a greater purpose in her life. As she started to believe that her great love was still out there, she began to have a greater faith in being just as happy again with a new man.

But what she also did was change the vibration she sent out to the universe.

Sydney ended up calling in the energy of a man who fulfilled most if not all of her core needs—and she had not just healed her karmic energy from past lives, but also those childhood wounds that were still affecting her emotional availability and vulnerability.

So while our catalyst love is not meant to last, the effect on us and our lives will be everlasting.

It's this love that finally frees us from our outdated story lines and the belief that we have to accept less than we deserve. It's about realizing that love doesn't come the way we think it will and that maybe, just maybe, there's more to life than being in a relationship, anyway.

No one can bring about change in our life more than our

beautiful catalyst love, and therefore, even if they were a twin flame imposter—we can still forever be grateful for the experience.

ENDING THE CYCLE ONCE AND FOR ALL

Our karmic love comes into our life solely to teach us valuable lessons.

Not to last forever, not to be the answer to our prayers or our Prince Charming, but to slowly and deliberately pull apart the fabric of our lives so that we then have no choice but to change, to grow, and to eventually transition into being receptive to our forever love.

The first lesson we have to acknowledge during this phase is that not every love is supposed to last. We have to let go of thinking that it's in our control somehow, and if only we talked more, had sex more, gave more, then this relationship would magically turn into everything we've ever wanted. We also must make peace with our ego as well. We must admit to ourselves that no matter how amazing we are, no matter how loving or good, we can't make someone re-ciprocate what we extend toward them.

We can't make someone want to do better, and we can't make a relationship last whose sole purpose was to end so that we could move on.

The second and perhaps more difficult lesson is learning to cope with the fear of what happens if this love does end. Love is hard. No one is debating that. For many of us, we must block out the possibility of it ending in order to even try again. It's natural to be afraid of ending up alone, whether it's just the idea of being alone, or a more specific image of what it would mean for our self-worth if no one claimed us as theirs.

We must become so comfortable with ourselves that we do not strive to be with someone just out of loneliness or fear.

This third phase of the karmic love is called "the lesson" for a reason: we truly are learning during this stage. We're learning how to see things as they are and not as we wish they were; we're learning to observe unhealthy behavior; and we're gradually learning how to put ourselves first. From an early age we are taught to not be selfish, especially as women, and that in love we should always be selfless—putting others' needs before our own.

This only ends in mental and emotional depletion, however, never self-fulfillment.

Before we learn these important life lessons, we seem to think it's better to be with someone than to be alone, even if that someone isn't treating us particularly well. Part of this stems from the cultural norm in which we are still expected to grow up, pair off, marry, and reproduce; the other aspect is that, socially speaking, we have a very couples-based society—even when traveling, we are given rates for double occupancy. Being single is still seen as a difficulty rather than a choice. This stereotype and frame of mind is shifting, but only very recently; it's still something that as a whole we are going to need to experience in order to truly change our overall expectations and the relationship paradigm.

Growing through our three loves isn't just about having two relationships before we get to the one where we finally have the big white wedding and live happily ever after. It's about shifting the consciousness of our society. When we have large numbers of people becoming aware and going through the lessons of their soul mate and karmic loves, then we also have people who are waking up, healing themselves, and in turn creating change around them.

This phase is about us becoming better people and about letting the love we experienced make us better regardless of whether or not it has lasted.

ACCEPTANCE MEANS FREEDOM

Once we accept that something is different from what we had hoped or wished it would be, we set ourselves free from thinking that it could have been anything other than what it is.

So, for that big final lesson, we're going to have to get to the place where we can see the value of a relationship, of love, even if we're betrayed in the end.

Even if our karmic love crashes and burns (which in all likelihood it will), we have to get to that place where we're not acting in retaliation or anger, but can actually step back, take responsibility for our actions, be accountable for our part in the unhealthiness of the relationship, and extend forgiveness to our ex and to ourselves. To practice these steps is not only the biggest lesson, but also the one that will clear any remaining karma and put you in place to move forward, ready for your forever love.

We know we have succeeded in moving on when we can retain the lessons without bitterness or a closed heart. This isn't to say that we are explaining or excusing the bad behavior of either our partners or ourselves, though it may look like that to the outside world. The difference is, not only will the cycle have ended, but because we have acknowledged and healed the karma, that intense connection or attraction will be severed—the soul tie will be cut. A soul tie is another way of describing this connection because we're literally connected through lifetimes—not because we're meant for each other, but because we hold each other's key to becoming our higher selves.

With most karmic loves, the way we can tell if karma truly has been cleared is that once it has, while we may still find that other person attractive or not mind not talking to them, we won't have that "how can I get his attention, I want to rip off our clothes" feeling. This acceptance is a sign of growth and healing.

In order to truly absorb the lessons of this relationship and not shut down for future love, we must get to the place where we have peace with our ex-partner, which fully occurs once the relationship has officially ended and both people have had time to breathe and think about things.

Unfortunately, this means that the breakup for this connection is more drawn out than that of the soul mate. We will linger in that gray area of "are we together or not" for some time, still being intimate and on most mornings unsure of whether we are in love or hate with our partner.

Alyssa wanted her karmic love to be her twin flame. She wanted it to be something that was meant to last forever, not necessarily because it was healthy but because he was familiar, and she had fallen in love not just with him but with their story line.

It didn't matter when her partner, Caleb, told her up front that they weren't twin flames. She still believed they were, still thought that he'd change his mind and come to see the truth.

Alyssa was afraid of what would happen if she admitted that he wasn't her twin flame. It would mean that the inconsistent behavior and betrayals wouldn't have a purpose, in her mind, and that she was in just another shitty relationship that she had glorified because she wanted it to work.

She came to me when she didn't know what else to do.

Ultimately, like so many of us, Alyssa was afraid of moving on. She didn't know what it would entail, and so it became easier to keep ignoring all the reasons why Caleb wasn't her twin flame, why the relationship was unhealthy. In the process, she was having to stuff her needs down, lie to herself, and act in ways that she knew were not part of who she really was.

Eventually, she found the strength to cut things off with him. While she missed Caleb and still longed for him, ultimately she felt free.

She felt like she had just passed the biggest test of her life.

As we become less afraid of moving on and start to value our own peace of mind, we will get to the place where none of that matters to us any longer, because instead of giving to us, the relationship only feels like it's taking from us. We come to feel that if we were to continue any sort of relationship with our karmic love, we would have to forget everything that we know to be true—our worth, what we deserve, our intuition, and our self-love.

In short, it will come down to the decision between our karmic relationship or ourselves, our own inner peace and the love that we have for ourselves.

To get to the place where we are strong enough to choose ourselves, though, also means that we have and are in the process of healing our own wounds, those aspects of our soul that bled on others because we hadn't wanted to tend to them properly. This is why this love is so amazing: it takes the harshest road possible, but it also allows us to heal our past wounding, familial conditioning, and karma—but only by choosing ourselves.

CHOOSING OURSELVES ABOVE ALL OTHERS

If we don't choose ourselves, no one else will either.

We do heal, grow, and not only become more of who we truly are, but we also heal all those things about ourselves that had been holding us back from vulnerability and true intimacy. Our twin flame won't reveal themselves to us until we have healed, until we are ready for them, and until we are vibrating on a similar energy wave. In order to get to that place, we have to make the most of the lesson phase of our karmic love so that we don't move on to someone similar under the guise of having healed.

Once we have admitted that we are in a karmic love, or even just highly suspect it based on the reality phase, the next step is to end things—but we don't have to stop loving them. We can end things purely because they are no longer healthy, even when it's unlikely that they ever were. We can tell our partner that we love them even as we break up with them; we can extend healing and positivity to them—but it doesn't mean we have to keep things as they have been or keep accepting the status quo.

While you are guaranteed there will be a blowout at the end of this love, it doesn't have to end on a bad note. That, however, depends greatly on how able we are to do our own work. When we use this phrase *do our own work*, which seems to be gaining popularity, it means that we are basically looking at our shit too. To do our own work means that we're trying to figure out why we keep dating older men, or why we don't like to spend the night after we have sex, anything that gets in the way of having a truly open, healthy, high-functioning relationship with another.

To do our own work means we're not making excuses or participating in the same patterns or cycles; it means that we're not blaming everything on another person or our parents. We would be hard pressed to find someone who didn't think there was something difficult or traumatic about their childhood, but that doesn't mean as adults we can still use that as an excuse for our current behavior. Some of us have experienced truly horrific events growing up—abuse, or the death of a parent—but we also all have the ability to heal as well, and life isn't about saying "my pain was worse than yours" or "my life is harder now than yours, so I'm entitled to behave this way; I'm entitled to act this way because look how big and bad my wound is."

Doing our own work and healing says that we're all damaged to a degree, we've all been hurt, we've all had our trust broken, but the growth occurs when we say, "Enough!"

Choosing ourselves means that our own healing is a priority.

It begins the moment we say that just because it's always been this way doesn't mean it has to continue. It begins when we can say, no, it wasn't right that we were treated the ways we were by those who said they love us, but it also doesn't mean that we have to let that prevent us from moving forward.

We deserve healing, we deserve forgiveness, and we deserve to know without a doubt that we are worthy of the highest form of love regardless of what was done by us or to us in our past. What we learn through this process is that by forgiving them—we also forgive ourselves.

We can forgive ourselves for needing to go through this experience, for having a hand in breaking our own hearts, and for accepting less than we know we deserve.

When we can stay present in the moment and aware of what is going on without taking on victim mentality, then we can look at the ending of our karmic love with different eyes. We can see codependency as the fear of being left; we can see cheating as being a test to see if we will stick up for our needs; lying becomes a lesson for us to express our own truth; and betrayal is the ultimate test of forgiveness. To do our work means we take out the personal from this relationship; it means things aren't being done to us, and if we don't take it personally, we can then look purely at what we can gain from the experience.

Even the most brutal betrayal can have the most beautiful lessons. Hannah had been with a man who she thought might have been her twin flame. They had a connection that was out of this world, sex so good it was beyond reason, and no matter what seemed to happen she could just never cut the cord of this relationship. It didn't matter that they were both in relationships when they met, or that he continued to be involved with his child's mother while they were supposedly beginning their relationship.

None of it mattered because she always found an explanation for his behavior, she always believed it was for a reason and, ultimately, she always thought their love was strong enough to one day be what she had felt it could be from day one.

Of course, this was her first mistake—thinking that she just had to put in the time, like a jail sentence, in order to have the relationship she knew she deserved. But that's the journey we make when we embark on love, and so it was exactly what she needed to experience. At the end of their relationship, however, after she had handed him complete control of her finances, after they'd traveled together, made plans for the future, spoken of their love, and after she had basically financially supported him for over a year, he took off on a whim, across the country to pursue happiness with another woman.

To say her heart was broken is an understatement.

This wasn't just a relationship to Hannah, it was her whole life, and this man whom she had built up as being her forever love left her heart in tatters and her unsure if she even believed in love any longer. When I first met her, she was still angry with him, as I am sure any of us would be. In fact, I think she wasn't just angry, but "Angela Bassett setting the car on fire in the 1995 movie *Waiting to Exhale*" angry: it was an entirely different level.

She wasn't shy about doing the work or owning her part, either.

She admitted that she ignored the warning signs, that she purposely didn't ask questions of him because she was afraid of the truth, and that deep down, she felt he was involved with another woman.

She began to process not just the breakup but the entire relationship. She admitted that, as an empath, she did exhibit some codependent qualities, and that while she hoped her ex wasn't a full-blown narcissist, he did show some related behaviors. She admitted to being okay with being the other woman because she still wasn't sure if she had enough to give to a full relationship, and ultimately, she concluded that while his behavior was unacceptable, she had participated in what had happened. She finally ended by closing down the connection because of her quest for peace of mind and self-love, but never did her love for this man diminish.

She simply became rooted in the realization that she deserved better than he was capable of, and that she was immensely grateful for all they had experienced. And so she forgave him, told him she loved him, and moved on into her healing.

Perhaps we aren't all immediately capable of forgiving and moving forward in that way, but it is something that we can all journey toward. Sometimes we hear the term, "They don't deserve to be forgiven"—but what we're really saying is that we don't deserve forgiveness as something to do for ourselves and our healing. Forgiveness shifts our action away from the other person. We don't have to decide whether or not the person deserves our forgiveness, we give it to ourselves in order to release ourselves from the pain and move forward.

No other relationship tests our ability to forgive like that of our karmic love, in part because they hold our wounded hearts promising to love us better, promising to do what they couldn't with their soul mate, promising to grow with us—and they did, it just wasn't in the way that we had hoped.

We can love someone forever while still knowing that we're not meant to actually be in relationship with them because there's only one relationship that is meant to last. There's only one love—and relationship—that is supposed to last, everything else is just a beautiful lesson, a compass pointing us in the direction of our forever.

The Third *Love,*
Our Twin Flame

THE ONE THAT JUST FEELS RIGHT

PART I

THE DREAM

Love Is Always Worth the Work

A broken heart can't ever imagine loving again, yet love has a way of sneaking in without us knowing or inviting it. We doubt that it's love at times because it feels different and in many ways makes us question if we ever even loved before. Sometimes we have a difficult time accepting our third love simply because our experience of love so far has involved pain and difficulty.

No one ever sets out looking for their twin flame; there's no dating app that magically lets us find the person with whom we share the same fire, this person who somehow, while not perfect themselves, is perfect for us. At first, we tend to not believe or fully invest in this relationship because during this first phase of twin flame love, we indeed see them as being perfect.

Love has only ever shown us that we have to sacrifice, to work and work, even when we know in our hearts that it isn't actually making us happy. While the idea of twin flames is becoming more widely known and accepted, it still seems like a bit of a fairy tale. We think, sure, that sounds wonderful but it's just a romantic idea—not something that can happen in real life.

In truth this romance is such a whirlwind that in order to actually begin to understand it, we have to suspend our entire belief system about what we think love should look like. Is this love amazing? Yes. Is it always easy? No. But having an easy relationship isn't the point.

Twin flames are highly connected spiritual relationships, the kind of love that we often refer to when we speak about meeting our other half or even The One. It is believed that back in the time when the universe was created, each of us had a twin flame with whom we shared a single force of energy.

Over the course of several lifetimes, we were reincarnated in different bodies and roles, sometimes male or female, mother or child, siblings, or even friends, so that we could learn different lessons that would help each soul rise through the various levels of consciousness, until finally we are joined together.

It's sometimes difficult to take in the meaning of the twin flame relationship, especially when we have been conditioned to think that relationships are really just an end in and of themselves: marriage and growing old with someone. While twin flames can do these things, what separates this type of relationship from all others is that the purpose of it transcends the well-being of the two parties to in fact make a difference in the world at large.

THE MISSION OF UNCONDITIONAL LOVE

Apart from the higher purpose of this kind of love, the most important factor is that this love is unconditional, which separates this connection from the karmic.

While karmic love is responsible for clearing our karma from lifetimes past, our twin flame's mission is to teach us the meaning and action of unconditional love. Sometimes called *agape* (ah-GAH-pay), it's the highest form of love that we can experience on earth. It's extending love toward our partner without any expectations or stipulations—in other words, unconditional.

This relationship is ultimately destined to not just end with warm nights cuddled up in bed but with us becoming more of the person that we were born to be. It's the relationship that will lead us back to ourselves, and while perhaps the methods are sometimes challenging, it's also one that is invaluable because no one can do for us what our twin flame can. It's the journey to not just extend unconditional love for our partner but also for ourselves and those around us; it's to truly feel not just the emotion of love, but to become the vibration.

Unconditional love transcends reality, it stretches across time and overcomes the impossible. It's also the love that says "I love you simply because you're you" not "I love you only if you return love to me." It's learning that we can love someone and accept all of them without trying to make them be something or do something that is not authentically right for them.

This is why this love feels so easy in the beginning, so wonderful and even so free. We don't have to do anything to earn this love, we don't have to love bomb or impress, we don't even have to sacrifice any part of ourselves—all we have to do is simply be.

Before we meet our twin flame, many of us have already become comfortable being alone. We're happy with *me* and at times we don't even necessarily care if we end up in a relationship again. So when we first meet this special person, we don't have expectations attached to this relationship, we don't have milestones we want to reach, like marriage or children—we're simply enjoying the presence of this person, wherever the experience leads.

It feels easy because the unconditional love is there from the beginning, even if eventually the relationship will require work.

While many of us say that we unconditionally love someone, it's much more difficult in practice. This is why we undergo multiple lessons and phases in order to get to that place where we not only understand love but also have embodied it.

Where it's not just about *feeling* love—but *being* love.

JUST LET IT BE

One of the important factors in the twin flame dynamic is that we don't try to make it be something that it's not.

We let the relationship reveal itself to us, and in the process, the relationship takes shape organically.

We have all heard of *pheromones*, scents that we subconsciously pick up from others that either draw us in or repel us. Vibrations work in a similar way, and like radio stations, we all vibrate on different frequencies—the difference with twin flames is that they are on the same frequency, the same energy level.

This is likely something that we won't even be able to describe about this person in the beginning, but we will just feel that there is a knowing of each other, a comfort level that surpasses any previous relationship. Twin flames naturally have a higher level of vibration even before meeting, so this results in that magical pull that we have toward them, no matter how illogical it may seem.

Not only do we have our own unique vibration with each other, but the emotions that we experience do as well. If we are angry, jealous, selfish, sad, or even struggle with low self-confidence, we will vibrate lower, whether that's our normal frequency or not; yet the same is true for emotions like serenity, happiness, acceptance, a healthy self-image, and of course love. These are the highest vibrating emotions. So as we move through this process and finish healing the wounds from our karmic partner, our vibration will increase.

Once we begin practicing mindfulness, which is the act of staying centered in the moment and in control of our thoughts, we will embody more and more of the love frequency that is really the purpose of this entire connection.

An interesting aspect of this connection is that it will challenge us in so many ways so that we can grow, usually in ways we least expect. Thus, our twin flame will likely be someone we never expected to be with, even someone we would have first categorized as being all wrong for us.

It's not uncommon for our twin flame to be from a different racial, cultural, or socioeconomic background; it's also not unheard of to have a significant age difference as well. Twin flames can reincarnate as the same gender, even if one is the masculine soul and the other feminine. This occurs not to be an obstacle but rather to have us learn that the best kinds of love usually come packaged in ways that we would never have imagined, and to clear any lingering personal or familial conditions about who our ideal partner would be.

Even if it's not in such a drastic fashion, most twin flames comment that their twin was nothing like "their type."

This sentiment is echoed in the 2018 movie *Crazy Rich Asians*, where Rachel (Constance Wu) finds out that her longtime boyfriend Nick (Henry Golding) is actually very rich. She first discovers this on board a flight back to his home in Singapore for a family wedding (their seats aren't just in first class, but in "luxury" class). Rachel is surprised and, as an NYU professor, never anticipated or desired to date a man who is as wealthy as Nick. It doesn't change her feelings about him, but she sees a new version of him once they arrive overseas.

Like any good New Yorker, Rachel is adaptable and quickly grows accustomed to this new life that she previously wasn't aware of and that wasn't part of her story about what her type was.

During the film, we move through several key moments in which Rachel first must learn how to fit in with one of Singapore's richest families—but then we see a crisis develop between Rachel and Nick's mother, Eleanor (Michelle Yeoh). Eleanor makes it known that Rachel is not enough for her son Nick and that she vehemently disapproves of their relationship. While it seems that Rachel and Nick may be doomed, in one of the final scenes Rachel meets with Eleanor and tells her that she will back away because of how much she loves Nick. She sweetly reminds his mom that one day, when Nick is happily married to another woman she's approved of, it will be because of Rachel's ability to let her love go, for the sake of his own happiness.

Of course, in the end, Eleanor comes around, and Rachel and Nick seem to find their forever love. The movie also illustrates that we have to abandon the journey we have laid out in our mind when we expect to find love, because it never comes packaged as we would imagine it to.

In order to truly embrace this kind of love, we must understand that nothing will make sense: how this person looks, what the connection and attraction feel like, and even the timing of it. Nothing will follow any sort of traditional time lines or even relationship standards. It's the love connection that truly is one of a kind, and while we can have multiple soul mates and karmic partners, we only ever get one twin flame, one connection that is unlike any other, and one person who only ever desires that we learn to love ourselves as deeply as they love us.

But it's not going to come packaged all pretty and convenient. It will likely be more like a wild hurricane, where life is forever marked by a before and after. While we may possibly meet this person in our twenties, it's unlikely that we will enter into a relationship with them until later in life.

This is because we wouldn't have been ready for them earlier.

In order to receive our twin flame, we need to have not only cleared a considerable amount of karma, but we need to have become more centered in who we are as individuals. We need to have traveled through our first and second loves so that we could heal our wounding. Otherwise, we would be treating our twin flame relationship just like any other and wouldn't even be aware of the uniqueness it possesses.

Jenna, for example, had crossed paths multiple times with her twin flame, both through work and social circles. But each time she did, she was still in the throes of her karmic love. She was addicted to that chaos and drama and didn't even notice Henry.

Not until years later, after she had divorced and been single for a while, did she realize that the universe had been throwing them together for some time—she just hadn't been ready for him.

While it may be necessary that we meet our twin flame later in life, that can also be part of the problem, because in the beginning, we may dismiss this relationship, this feeling, as an affair, that it is as amazing as it is because we haven't yet made a commitment. Telling ourselves this allows us to stay where we are, to not change, and ultimately to not have to rebuild our lives from the ground up, which is what this connection requires.

Because we have learned so much about who we are, we're no longer looking for another to make us whole. We feel confident, secure, and more than happy being alone. So when our twin flame enters the picture, there is no pressure to be anything other than what it is—a love that just feels easy.

A twin flame won't be perfect, there will be mistakes, but it's a connection that's going to inspire you.

LIFE WILL NEVER BE THE SAME AGAIN

While no relationship is perfect, the love that is present will still feel like it comes so easy.

Even if twin flames are in each other's lives for several years before, perhaps as associates, friends, coworkers, or even just a distant acquaintance, the feelings lie dormant. A knowing may be present, a connection, a familiarity or even a feeling that comes out when we lock eyes with our twin—we may intuitively feel that this person is of significance to us. But we disregard it because they are too young for us, or too old, or not from the right background or we tell ourselves we're happily married (right?).

Sometimes we even forget about this person altogether in the beginning, disregarding the feelings completely, telling ourselves that our lives are already planned and on track. We can see where we'll be five years down the road, where we'll be working, how long we'll be married, even where we may vacation.

But then there's a moment.

A tilting of the universe and somehow the impossible happens. We perhaps meet this person for the first time, or we suddenly are in a situation where our perspective has shifted, and we see them in a different light. Our guard falls just enough to let them in—and in that moment, life will never be the same again. Perhaps it occurred when we looked into the eyes of a teacher at our child's school, or we caught the gaze of a stranger across a bar while away for a girls' weekend. However it happens, in that moment we feel that all along life had been leading to this moment.

Whatever the specifics, life will not be the same, we will not be the same. Despite how hard we might try to deny it, we receive a glimpse of something that we never thought possible. Regardless of timing or the impossibility of it all, a connection was ignited that we won't ever be able to forget.

Twin flames have divine timing even if it first seems inconvenient for us.

Simone's world rocked when she met her twin flame while on vacation with friends, a yearly trip they made every winter. This particular year, however, the stars aligned, and she crossed paths with her twin flame. They met randomly, their other friends present, but immediately felt a pull to each other. It was as though they had known each other forever. That moment was the beginning of the journey for them.

While she embraced the feelings and significance earlier on than he did, the experience still constantly challenged her rational brain. After all, they were both married to other people—with children.

As far as Simone was concerned, she was happy with her life. Perhaps her marriage wasn't one she would have chosen later in life, but they loved each other, they had a family, and a life together. It never had occurred to her to get a divorce or to start a life on her own. The thing that Simone is still learning about the twin flame relationship is that it's truly a journey. Most romantic relationships consist of meeting each other, then in about six months, we've either realized it was just a fling and break up, or we've grown more serious and start the process of welding our lives together by introducing our partner to our families, moving in, or even becoming engaged.

Whether we're always aware of it or not, we tend to follow a recipe for love, the final product being marriage or some type of deep commitment.

Twin flames are different, of course, because nothing about this connection is normal or traditional. In fact, at different times during this journey, we will go through the process of being challenged in how we approach relationships and define commitment. The ultimate purpose of this connection is to grow, which means that in many scenarios this connection can take months or years to come to fruition.

The growth in this connection is different. Rather than healing our pasts, it's about being able to open up to our futures. It's less about who we are and more about the person we're meant to become. This doesn't mean that we won't be with our twin during this process, but it does mean that we must understand that the main priority of this connection is personal growth—the romantic relationship itself always comes second.

As the relationship with her twin progressed, Simone came to understand that she hadn't actually been happy or satisfied with her marriage for a very long time, but because it had happened so slowly, she had become used to the dissatisfaction. Ironically, the same was true for her twin flame as well, in a marriage where he adamantly would say he loved his wife, at times sounding like he was trying to convince himself.

So many of us talk ourselves into being—or at least remaining—unhappy.

We tell ourselves that this is just the way it is, we're adults now so we must put on our big girl (or boy) pants and deal with it, because no one is really happily in love, with an amazing sex life forever—right? Or at least this is the inner dialogue that we have with ourselves to avoid change.

In essence, we talk ourselves out of being happy, out of leaving a dying or dead relationship or marriage because of children, finances, the expectations of others, or even because we don't want to leave our comfort zone—and with regular run-of-the-mill affairs, that might work, but not with our twin flame because they won't quit until we start to get real with ourselves.

Until we begin to open our eyes and actually acknowledge the connection, the feeling, and that mind-blowing attraction that makes you feel as if you actually have lost your mind.

AWAKENED SEXUALITY

One of the signatures of twin flames is their physical attraction and sexual desire for each other.

Twin flames have an intense physical attraction toward each other because of that similar energy level, because of that comfort, and because sex with our twin flame transcends what we thought sex could be—often described as the best of our lives. It's not that it's just deeply making love, but also that there is an intense passion that doesn't occur with other romantic relationships, one that literally feels like an involuntary physical reaction every time we see them or even are just around them.

Karen also was married at the time of meeting her twin flame.

She described their meeting as "waking up" her sexuality. Before this, she would have said she had become a very unsexual person, that her sexuality and desire were dormant, and that maybe that's just what happens after having kids and being married for so long (it's amazing the lies we tell ourselves so that we can pretend being unhappy is normal). But when she met her twin, all that changed. She even described the tingling she had between her legs and the feeling that "Oh my god, I can feel something," literally in shock that she was having sexual desires—just from being around him.

This attraction isn't only because we are drawn to the way that they look or even the person they are, but arises because it's a soul-to-soul attraction. It's the feeling of being truly seen by another and having them see and fully accept us; that unexplainable feeling that another person just "gets" us, when we had long since given up on the idea that it was even possible.

Twin flames also emphasize the aspect of sex being an energy exchange. I've talked with several women who remark that they never even knew what sex was until it was with their twin flame. Like Stacey said, "Sex with him is like finally realizing what the big hype has been about the whole time." It's the expression of the deep soul-to-soul connection, but it's also about the multidimensional attraction that we feel with them.

What this also teaches us is that there is a difference between a person who can turn us on physically versus turn us on spiritually or even mentally. Because the twin flame connection is one that truly is a mind-body-soul connection, the attraction exists on every level. We're not just wanting to strip them naked and jump into bed with them, we want to be close to them, to talk to them, to sit quietly together just enjoying each other's presence.

It's not only a sexual chemistry; it's a sense of wholeness or completeness. That's why no matter how much or for how long we resist this connection, we will always be led back to each other.

Once a soul finds its home, it never truly forgets.

THE SLOW BURN

Twin flames always know the perfect time to come into each other's lives.

Whether it's at the end of a marriage or after years of self-healing, it always seems to happen when it's supposed to, even if at times it may feel inconvenient or challenging.

As humans, we like to control (or at least to live within the illusion that we can control) our lives and what occurs, when in truth much of life simply happens. But because this love feels so easy in the beginning, we tend to categorize it in a way we're more comfortable with.

We place a label on it and then try to move forward. Sometimes it's friends—"we're just friends" I've heard so many say to me. But just as we can't make a relationship romantic if those feelings aren't there, we can't pretend a connection is just a friendship when stronger feelings are present.

Sometimes in these situations, we don't want to label anything, we just want to see what happens because we've had our hearts broken so many times before. So instead of jumping the gun, we start off as "friends" and see where it goes, not knowing that we're building our Five Foundations in the process.

While the physical attraction is there from day one, it's unlikely that we'll jump into being in a relationship right away. Not because the feelings aren't present but because we're okay with not forcing anything this time around.

Annie met her twin flame, Robert, on a run one Saturday morning. She describes the connection as her being just naturally drawn to this man. The first few moments of conversation with him made her feel like she had been talking with him for years.

The instant knowing was present.

They got together for a hike the following weekend and I remember her saying, "Even then it felt like we were together, like we have always been together." It's been a couple years since that first date, and they are still making the most of every moment. They've had their challenges, but through it all, the love, acceptance, and support have been so strong there hasn't been anything they couldn't get through.

But this time Annie didn't rush it. She didn't try to announce a relationship on social media or get him to pinpoint their status right away. She interviewed him, she took her time, and ultimately she let the relationship be what it was meant to be.

Ultimately this phase is about letting in this love, experiencing the powerful connection that's present, and then taking that knowledge and reflecting on it for ourselves.

The decision to continue to let things progress with our twin flame is hugely important because it reflects the amount of personal growth that we've experienced so far. Even if we want to take our time, even if we're not rushing to have another complete us, we still have to make that conscious choice to stay connected. We have to decide that we're ready for it.

We can't choose our twin flame until we, in fact, choose ourselves. Until we do, we can't actually commit to the journey that this connection requires, we can't trust being led in a direction we couldn't ever have imagined, and we can't actually choose the love of our twin flame, because, being of the same vibration, they feel our very doubts and hesitations.

Being with our twin flame isn't just about a romantic relationship, it's about a life.

READY FOR LOVE

Being ready for love means we're ready to do things differently this time.

No matter how many challenges are present, though, no matter if distance or marriages or other kinds of social divides separate twin flames, they will always find a way to come together because when they are in each other's physical presence, the rest of the world disappears. Time stops, and we're reminded that, for the best things, there just aren't words to explain.

Twin flames move through various phases that are part of the overall journey. While some are amazing and earth-shattering, like when we first meet or kiss, others are difficult because we just want them with us, to enjoy each other and that love that feels like it's almost too easy.

There are always spaces that are meant to occur within this connection. Sometimes it's about a physical geographic separation; at others, it's about knowing there's more healing that needs to occur before coming together. But the awareness is present, and both twins will guide each other on this journey. It won't be through unhealthy behaviors or abuse, but through the true desire to help each other become their best selves.

These spaces are often referred to as the *runner and chaser* phase of the twin flame connection: where one twin, usually the masculine, out of fear deserts the feminine. Either he stays in his current relationship and ignores her, or he sabotages the relationship by having an affair. Either way, it's the same—he rejects the connection, at least for the time being.

This type of behavior is just one example of how a twin flame relationship can resemble the karmic passion and how we can excuse and romanticize a karmic love as our twin flame.

Because of the healing both twins have done, however, a twin flame will never completely desert you. They may not be ready to fully commit because they still have soul work to do. But they will find themselves drawn back to their twin flame partner.

Being ready for love means that we're ready for the reality of it—not just the dream.

It means that, while this love came in so unexpectedly, we're still going to have to work to make it a reality or rearrange our lives to make that happen. A twin flame will never force you to accept less than you deserve or treat you with narcissist behavior patterns, consciously or otherwise—but they still will challenge you.

They will still be able to help you heal even further.

Maria came to me after just meeting her twin flame, wondering, "If this is my twin flame, why doesn't it feel easier?" She was confused because he called her out on her behavior and made situations more difficult. But on reflection, she was able to see that her partner, Patrick, was helping her heal even further after her karmic love.

By asking questions and holding her accountable to herself, he was encouraging her healing process.

It's easy to think we're ready for our forever love until we're actually looking into its eyes and seeing exactly how our lives will change. Maybe that's why the words of Nicholas Sparks in his novel *The Notebook* rang so true. In the book, Noah screams to Allie, "So, it's not gonna be easy. It's gonna be really hard. We're gonna have to work at this every day, but I want to do that because I want you. I want all of you, forever, you and me, every day." In this romantic novel, Sparks describes the love between two people that time didn't even stand a chance in destroying, but it also showed that just because the love comes easy doesn't mean everything else will.

And perhaps that's the biggest lesson we learn during this phase: maybe it's not the love we have to work at, but rather getting to the space where we can just enjoy it.

PART II

THE REALITY

We Never Knew True Love Until Now

When something is meant to work, there's nothing that can stop it—not even ourselves.

Each one of us, no matter how cynical, dreams of love. Not just an "I love you" relationship, but the kind of connection that is truly fulfilling, where our hope within love is reignited, and we look into the eyes of our partner knowing without a doubt that there is no other person on this earth who could love us the same way, who could come into our lives and make it what they do.

It's a love that overcomes anything and keeps proving itself long after we've tried to throw away hope.

Twin flames are real. It is a connection that defies logic or even expectations, but that doesn't mean it's going to be easy and it doesn't mean that we are always ready for what this relationship brings into our lives—or the ways that our life is meant to change because of it.

LETTING LOVE FIND YOU

When I am speaking with clients about this connection, I always describe it as the relationship that occurs naturally because of the growth and soul work that each person is doing independently. While it's our similar vibration that originally draws us to this person, it's also that same feeling that can have us wanting to run in the opposite direction, even if only temporarily. The most important thing to understand about twin flames is that this relationship will not act or look like any sort of romantic connection we've ever had.

There will be no time lines, no following of the rules, or even abiding by any of the traditional milestones that we normally follow in relationships.

It's a love that is purely felt for love's sake.

The ultimate purpose of twin flame dynamics is to wake us up and help us become the people that we are meant to be. Yes, it's to enjoy an amazing partnership and love—but we're also going to grow because of the connection. When we first meet our twin, it can seem like a perfect love, one that we will never have to struggle through or even have issues that would cause us to disagree or argue. It feels so divinely orchestrated that we can't imagine ever getting to the point where we would separate or hurt the other person because even if love isn't vocally expressed in the beginning, it is still always felt.

We've learned, though, that regardless of how amazing something feels, we can't and no longer want to make it into something it's not meant to be. So even after considerable time together, twins will frequently still just be taking one day at a time.

This is a love that finds you because you've stopped searching for love—and because finally you are ready for love.

You've decided to focus on you and to enjoy your life as is; your life is full to the brim, even if you might not currently have a plus one. This is different from being closed to love, though, because you are open—you're no longer feeling like you're less of a woman just because you are not currently next to a man.

Kayla was happily single. She had healed from her karmic love, established good boundaries with her son's father, and felt that she was on the way to knowing herself. She made self-care a priority and took time to be mindful about what it meant to be in a relationship—but she wasn't looking for one.

She had decided simply to not focus on her relationship status any longer. For as long as she could remember, she had either been in a relationship, getting over a relationship, or trying to figure out how to get into another relationship.

So she decided that this time, while she felt ready for love, she wasn't going to focus on it.

And then in walked Mark. They had worked together occasionally in the past, but she never felt that spark—until one particular conference. Suddenly they just knew that they were connected. Yet neither one of them forced anything, and while they have an amazing relationship, it is currently long-distance.

So maybe she had decided she was ready for love—but she also let it find her.

They know that they still have challenges ahead of them, as they know they want to at least live in the same city rather than on opposite sides of the country, but they're not forcing it, they're not rushing it.

They're simply enjoying the process—regardless of where it leads.

LEARNING TO RECEIVE

Wanting something is different from having our arms—and our heart—open wide to receive it.

Up until this point we have become used to the love-bombing extreme highs and lows of our karmic love, so we've lost perspective on what it means to actually have a healthy relationship.

We now need to reframe how we think about relationships—and let go of our addiction to dysfunction.

We not only have to have learned all of those important lessons from our karmic relationship, but we have to be able to put them into practice. We have to get to the place where we can consciously receive our twin flame, and the stability and presence that they offer.

Imani was used to success. She ran an international business and had become very comfortable and confident in her own space. She had healed the abandonment issues that had risen because of her karmic love, and she was ready for a new relationship.

She had no desire to go looking for her twin flame, but she did want a man to treat her as she knew she deserved—something she had never previously asked for. On one of our calls, she mentioned Trevor, a man she had met while away the previous week.

She was hesitant to admit that right off the bat there had been a strong emotional and spiritual connection, but she couldn't deny it either. She was honestly surprised by the intensity of what she felt for Trevor but was excited nonetheless to be in this process with him.

It didn't take long for her to call me, upset.

Imani, like so many women, has trouble receiving and accepting what it is she says she wants. She didn't know what to do with his attention or sweet gestures, and more important, she didn't know how to handle a chaos-free relationship!

While feeling worthy of great love, she was still unsure how to accept it.

She and Trevor continued their relationship together, slowly but—most important—honestly. After she and I spoke, she decided to talk to him about what she was experiencing. That proved to be what she really needed. She simply needed to communicate her resistance so that she didn't feel she was in it alone, and so he would understand what she was going through.

By speaking about it, she found she was open to receiving more.

GROWTH IS ALWAYS THE GOAL

While we have done so much growing prior to meeting our twin flame, this relationship will ask more of us than any other. The choice to be transparent, accountable, and to steer clear of previous patterns or cycles isn't always easy!

Twin flame relationships will go through many different stages during the journey. The first phase is awareness, when twin flames first meet and experience the love they can't stay away from no matter how hard they try. Suddenly we are so deep in, we can't imagine our life without the other person, which then scares us because up to this point, everyone who said they'd always be there for us has left.

Until now, every time we've whispered "forever" to a partner, love has only shown to be fleeting, never really able to withstand the storms that life will inevitably bring.

Of course, this is also because most relationships are intended to teach us lessons, not actually last forever. But this is hard to keep in mind when we are feeling that intense chemistry that twin flames are known for.

Now the lesson is that a relationship can last forever and also be that vehicle for immense growth.

During the awareness and connection phase in the beginning, we not only start to grow in love with our twin, but our souls begin to come together. While we have come to reject the idea of The One because we feel whole on our own, when we meet our twin and we start to feel that crossing over of energy, we can't help but feel that everything we've experienced so far has led to this moment.

During this process we're asked to believe not only that love can last, but that it can help us grow without simultaneously hurting us as well. We have to learn that growth doesn't always mean tears and pain, but also long conversations and unconditional love.

This is the love that makes all other loves irrelevant; the one that shows us why it didn't work out with anyone before; but it's also going to challenge any belief about love and unravel anything that we are still grasping onto for comfort.

Forever love isn't always a pretty picture, and it's not going to flatter us or tell us what we want to hear. It's not going to fit in that little box and abide by any sort of rules. In fact, it's going to continually challenge us on every level as to whether this even is love.

Not because this is a mind game that once again traps us, but because we need to understand that even in absences, even in turmoil, chaos, disappointment, or sadness—unconditional love is still present.

Ava contacted me because she was scared that she was becoming too dependent on Keith, the man that she suspected was her twin flame. She had been through her soul mate love and her karmic love, and now was trying so hard to do things differently.

Keith was incredible from the start. He was patient and had no problem expressing his interest in and attraction to her. They would go for long drives and talk about things she'd never talked about with anyone else. He challenged her beliefs, but in ways that made her think, not doubt herself, as had always happened in the past. But because things were going so well, she started to wonder if she was falling back into old patterns of codependency.

In the past, Ava admitted, she'd had a difficult time getting over someone once they had broken up. She was in love with Keith, but she was afraid of being destroyed if he left. She couldn't imagine picking up the pieces of her broken heart yet once again.

Through our talks, she came to realize that it wasn't just about receiving this wonderful man into her life but about recognizing that the triggers his challenges set off were doing good. She was continuing to grow and explore her independence within a relationship. Once she could see that being scared wasn't necessarily a negative aspect to the relationship but a way she could grow even further, she allowed herself to learn the lesson that it was okay to need someone.

It's a love that not only triggers us but also helps us grow in unconditional love for ourselves and our partner.

EVEN TWIN FLAMES MAKE MISTAKES

We say that we aren't going to romanticize love anymore. We say that we understand that no relationship is perfect. Yet when we're first tested by our twin flame, it can often make us question everything we thought we knew about love.

The second phase of the twin flame relationship is when we are tested, when it seems like we are the biggest obstacle to being together, not because we don't love each other but because we're afraid, because we doubt ourselves, and we're still battling the feelings of whether we deserve this love or not. While we are meant to learn to have faith without self-sacrifice and to trust our own feelings and inner knowing, we also at times have to overcome feeling unworthy or undeserving of a love like this.

Twin flames will never be perfect, but the relationship will always be worth it.

Nikki and her twin flame had an on-again, off-again relationship for years. As she progressed through the phases of the relationship, she made the choice to show up more for herself and to face what she was going through; she let herself be changed by the experience of loving her twin flame.

Her twin flame, despite how much work he had done and how much he loved her, couldn't quite give up that feeling that he didn't deserve her. His test was to overcome his past feelings of guilt and inadequacy so that he could be fully in a relationship with her.

It's never just one twin who is working through their own issues. While one twin works at their ego and confidence issues, the other may work through fear, vulnerability, and often issues of abandonment. Nikki had to stop being afraid that her twin would leave, because not only was that the vibration that she was sending out, but she also was accepting behavior she really wasn't okay with simply because she was scared that he would leave.

Over a period of several months, Nikki and her twin became better skilled in voicing their fears and were able to grow closer together and actually accept the love the other person was trying to offer them.

Even though each twin flame has a different set of issues they are meant to work through and heal, it doesn't mean that one wears a halo and the other doesn't. Twin flames have to master self-love in that delicate balance of giving to ourselves first because that is a direct reflection of what we'll be able to extend to another.

In this process, we have to love ourselves so fiercely that we no longer fear being left, and with that we give ourselves the ability to call bullshit when we see it instead of tiptoeing around it. We have to be honest when we're hurt or scared—we have to speak consciously about the things that matter, knowing that it's those moments that are going to bring us closer together.

This goes back to the overall vibration of the connection: while both twins were drawn to each other because of a similar frequency, if at any time that diminishes or changes based on their own internal struggle, then that changes their connection.

Communication is a vital part of keeping that vibration alive.

But even during these periods, the love is there, sometimes stronger than ever. Not just in a way that we felt it endearingly for our soul mate or even somewhat obsessively for our karmic love, but to a depth that we've never felt before. Both partners will have to accept this unconditional love, knowing that no matter what they do or what occurs, they will still be loved.

This is not a free pass for either twin to behave badly, knowing that the other person will always be there. Instead, they acknowledge the inner feeling that we deserve to be loved as much on our worst days as on our best.

Though the test phase may be difficult, it also means that twins are intimately connected even if the connection is not a traditionally defined relationship (which is rare for twin flames anyway). But it's during this phase that we're not just tested but able to glimpse the reward as well. In this case, the reward is when we start to see what it will be like to be in a relationship with our twin flame.

Our twin flame relationship is our reward for not just growing through our previous loves but for continually showing up for this process regardless of what it entails.

It's this sweetness that becomes imbedded in our hearts so that even when we're hurt, let down, or confused by the testing, we always come back to the love: the understanding and the feeling that somehow this other person gets us in a way that no one else ever has.

SURRENDER AND TRUST

Until now, we've never had the chance to completely surrender to a relationship and to trust not just the other person but the relationship itself.

We begin to believe that whatever is meant to happen will happen, and so there is no need to push or pull, play games or manipulate.

We begin to believe that love actually can last forever.

The final stage of this connection is surrender and union, when, after the tests and initial triggering, we come together stronger than before—but different because we're not in a rush, we're not worried that this love is going to up and leave tomorrow, we simply have surrendered to it and trust it.

People ask me about time lines—how long each phase might last. For instance, if phase one takes a year, will phase two take six months, and so on. This is one of the biggest confusions about twin flames: There are no time lines or expectations. Twin flame relationships not only refuse to follow a traditional relationship milestone such as dating, moving in together, and engagement, but will also disregard any actual measure of time.

A twin flame love is such because it is timeless.

We often are told if someone hasn't committed within six months, then we should move on. We are constantly bombarded with memes and articles from our girlfriends about how if he wanted to be with you, he would be, or how he's just stringing you along to keep you on the back burner. While that may have a place in dating and relationships, we can't really apply it to the twin flame connection.

Even though our other loves were soul contacts that we were meant to experience, this love is the coming together of two souls who originally and long ago were separated.

There are two different ways to describe time. The first is Chronos, or chronological time. This is how we measure time in our everyday lives: the minutes, hours, days, weeks, months, and even years. Yet this isn't how twins count time. Instead they operate on Kairos. Kairos is divine timing, the belief that everything happens the moment that it's meant to, and not a moment before. Now, we can't spin that to our boss as to why we were late for the umpteenth time this week, but Kairos is especially apt for twin flames.

When we're speaking of the journey of twin flames, we're also speaking about the role of our ego within the relationship. We can't completely disregard our ego or say it's a bad thing. Our ego exists because we exist: we need our ego for the way in which we think of ourselves, the space we take up in this world, and what we feel we deserve.

Confidence and ego are closely tied. While sometimes one substitutes for the other, in the ideal situation they work together, never competing, overinflating, or even self-deprecating each other. It's in the balance that we know our worth, but we don't think we're better than others. Healthy ego balance is knowing what we deserve but also what others and the world deserve from us.

These tests that twins experience during this time aren't frivolous, aren't just to see if we are over our karmic love; they are deeply seated in the healthy development of our ego. In our soul mate and karmic relationships, we can come together when we're a hot mess because, let's be honest, we all are at some point. But it doesn't work that way with our twin flames.

We only enter into the twin flame relationship when we're healed, grown, and able to truly sign on to forever.

What we often forget is that forever love isn't the same as a traditional relationship. We will feel that forever love long before we actually move in with our twin, long before we have any sort of defined commitment. We learn that it's not that beautiful diamond or piece of paper announcing us as husband and wife that guarantees forever, but rather the feelings that we just can't get rid of—regardless of how hard we try.

It's the kind of love that continually shows up against all odds, and it's this magic that makes twin flames what they are. In so many ways it's the possibility of being so hurt that makes this love also so incredible.

Stella loved love, no doubt about it. She and I had been working together for several years, and even in her worst moments, she'd say, "But I still believe, I believe not just in forever but that one person is meant for me." Her heart had been broken more times than I can count, but she always got right back up, always believed that her twin flame was just around the corner.

So I was surprised that when she finally found it—she no longer wanted it.

Over the course of one summer, Stella met Anthony and things had developed quickly, as they sometimes do with twin flames. They were able to be transparent and talk with one another, and were even planning a trip overseas for the autumn. They had just clicked and she knew that he was her one—"her lobster," as she called him, because that is one species that mates for life.

But when Anthony was suddenly called away for work for six months, Stella faltered.

I still remember her crying, saying, "I'm done, it's over, it was great while it lasted but I can't do that—I won't do that." For her, after being through so much romantically, she couldn't conceive of being part of a long-distance relationship. But sometimes what we learn is that just because we don't want to experience something doesn't mean that we're not meant to. She and I spoke in detail that night about surrender and trust. I said to her, "What will it really hurt to try? To trust him right now when he says this will work out? If you're hell-bent on having a broken heart, what's the difference if it's six months from now or tonight?" She reluctantly agreed, surrendered to what was happening, and tried her best to trust him in the process.

It wasn't easy and there were many moments she was ready to throw in the towel—but she never did.

They just celebrated the two-year anniversary of their first date and are happier and more fulfilled than they ever thought possible. What they both learned was that surrender and trust wasn't a one-time deal but something they continually practiced within the relationship. That has led not only to a stronger connection but also to feeling more at peace about whatever might happen in the future.

As we go through our romantic journey, we learn that the greater the love, the greater the chance of being hurt because we can't feel that amazing reward with a once-in-a-lifetime kind of love if it doesn't also have the ability to bring us to our knees. While this love feels unlike anything else, it takes a true commitment to ourselves in order to actually stay, show up, and do the work this connection requires of us, no matter how hard it may get.

This is why we say there are some loves that overcome every obstacle, that nothing can get in the way of, even ourselves, because to try to escape our twin flame is really to try to escape ourselves.

This time it's safe to trust. It's safe to tear down our walls for love.

PART III

THE LESSON

When It's Real, It Never Ends

Love only shows its true face over the course of time, through multiple obstacles, challenges, and even hurts. It's easy to say "I'll love you forever" after a few months or a year, but quite another to actually continue, even after we have every logical reason to close up, lock down, and throw away the key. When love is real, it never ends, it never wavers, and of course it never fails.

But just because love doesn't fail doesn't mean that we humans won't.

Twin flames are not only incredible but also indestructible: yet because we've been through countless heartbreaks before, we must learn this for ourselves and it's only something that we can see over time. It's seeing that no matter how many bad days we have, no matter how much we may fall back into self-sabotage or wounding, no matter how much we doubt—love never actually quits. It's this love that we must let ourselves warm up to, realizing that not only is this love, but this person isn't going anywhere.

By now we've learned that love doesn't come all prettily wrapped up like we expected it to, it doesn't fit into what we or our families have dreamed for us, and it will never ask us to give up who we are in order to make it work—but it does come. Twin flames are called our forever love because nothing can ruin that love or take it away. It is a love that was always there, it is we who must take the long road to understanding that.

During the reality phase of this love, we will hurt each other. The difference is that twins know exactly where to stick the knife; they know which wound needs to bleed in order to help us grow. They will be that mirror to us even when we wish they wouldn't. It is also during this phase that we begin to understand love is perhaps something even greater than we had previously thought.

Love is magical—perhaps it's the closest many of us ever get to true magic. Those feelings of sparks and connection, however, don't mean that we'll never have to get down and dirty in love. Love is magical because we have put in the hard work to make it that way: because we healed, and brought forth everything we believe is true about ourselves—and love.

That means our beliefs about what commitment is, who we are, and even what love means to us.

DEFINING OUR OWN FOREVER

Sometimes we just have to decide to do what feels right for us.

No matter how educated we are, many of us still dream of love in the traditional sense, even at this point in our lives. We still hear the word *forever* and we think white dresses, rings, and a ceremony at sunset. We start to think of monogrammed towels and his-and-her sinks. Even after everything we've been through, and we understand that this person who is our twin flame isn't going anywhere, we inevitably start to sink back into traditional ideas about forever love.

The lesson of twin flames love is to give up our idea of what a forever love is. It's to make that final break with conventionality and look at the love itself as the shimmering bond between two souls.

Only once we can do this may we see that the love is not necessarily as we envisioned it.

Society is moving farther away from expressing love in traditional ways, away from a one-size-fits-all love that we must cram ourselves into in order to have a life partner or be happy. But it's not easy. It's not easy because we're still bombarded by pictures of dream weddings when we check out at the market; it's not easy because we have been so programmed to think that forever means tradition. While we perhaps have let go of choosing a partner who fulfills certain requirements according to society, we now must look at what forever truly means for each of us.

Twin flames don't give a damn about cultural norms.

Claudia and Ray were twin flames that I met after they had

come together and were wondering what the next step was. They found each other later in life and opened a holistic school in Vermont together where they not only combined their preexisting families but also were doing something that they felt called to do. It was a way they felt they could share their love with the world.

But they were struggling to figure out how to define their togetherness.

They both had been married before and no longer felt like they wanted a traditional ceremony, but doing nothing didn't feel right to them, either. They wanted to celebrate their journey and the process that they had gone through to get to this point in a special way that felt right for them.

We spoke for a few months together until they decided that their children would "marry" them in a ceremony they created. It was outdoors, on a hill in late summer. Claudia wore a violet dress and their children asked them to promise to not just love each other, but them as well, joining both families together.

When we get right down to it, it's not a piece of paper that guarantees forever. It's not a wedding band and it's not even sharing a bed each evening. Forever love is there because it can't be anything else, because we have learned that while there are countless people on this planet, only one person has been able to reveal themselves as someone that we didn't want to—or even couldn't—exist without.

Often this unto-itself business is a scary proposition, especially because we hear it thrown around so casually: *"I can't live without you."* But what if we replaced *can't* with *don't want to*? What if we realized that not only are we better with each other, but our lives are as well?

WE ALL NEED SOMEONE

To accept that we don't want to be without a particular person is to also understand not only who we are but what we need from a romantic partner. Yet in order to reach this awareness, we also have to work our way through everything that came before it.

Other than perhaps with our soul mate love, which occurred before we really had our heart broken, we became afraid of saying "I need you." We hesitated to think or say that we were happier when someone special was around. We were reluctant to say "I miss you, it's been too long" because life happened and we became fearful. We didn't want to be seen as the infamous "needy" girl or guy, and of course it seems that not needing anyone has become the latest buzz phrase.

The whole idea of "I don't need you, but I want you" has somehow gotten out of context from what it actually means.

To truly absorb that this love is a forever love, to accept that this person isn't going anywhere, we also have to acknowledge to our lover that we need them. We must not see it as weakness, but as awareness. And most of all, we have to understand that to need another person doesn't mean that somehow we are less.

To need someone means that they fulfill something in our lives that no other does. To need someone means that they bring something to the table that no one else ever has. It might be tangible, such as helping us with our lives. But in terms of twins it could also mean that they give us an understanding we've never experienced before. It might feel like they help center us, that they keep us on course, or that in some ways we are more *ourselves* with them.

This is why we need the testing and the hurt during the reality phase, because while there are those rare third loves that come together quickly and never leave, we usually need to go without having someone around before we understand what they bring to our lives.

We can't actually commit to any relationship if we can't first see or admit that we need someone.

As I tell clients, we're not born into this world and then left to fend for ourselves in isolation. We need our parents or elders to care for us, both physically and emotionally, in order to survive and grow up. We need friends, siblings, and even coworkers to talk to, to sympathize with, to feel like someone has our back. We even need our employers or customers to continue our career or business so that we can have financial stability. We need our mechanic to fix what's wrong with the car. We need people, because no one is meant to go through this life completely alone—regardless of how it seems that might actually be an option at one time or another.

But even in the face of all that, to say we need our lover seems scary.

This is something that I understand firsthand. After so many broken hearts, I became reluctant to say that I needed anyone and took on my armor as an ultra-independent warrior chick. I was the first to say "I don't need you, but I want you" until I started thinking about what that meant and wondering if I was really being honest with myself.

It's also a shift from perspective. A few decades ago, women needed men to financially support them—but that has changed very rapidly. We no longer need to be provided for in the traditional sense, and so this space of what it means to need a partner from a conscious perspective is shifting as well.

For me it came down to what I can't buy or provide for myself. Do I need a man to pay for my next vacation? No. But do I need my partner to hold me close at the end of the day? Yes. Do I need the man in my life to support my dreams and be a protector? Yes.

What it came down to was realizing that I could still be independent, still be my wild warrior chick self—but also need the man who I was sharing my life with.

It sounds like we're saying we are dependent upon them when in reality it's just acknowledging the value that they bring to our lives. It's admitting that while only we are responsible for our happiness, our sense of self, we are brighter when they are around.

To say we need our lover, our twin flame, is to say, Yes, I am amazing, my life is amazing, but you make it even better. It's to say, Yes, I am whole, just as you are; but together, we are stronger, happier, more fulfilled than if we were apart, than if we were with another who lacked understanding or inspiration.

It's okay to need someone. It's okay to both want and need our lover, our twin flame. It doesn't make us weak, it doesn't make us somehow sound childish. In fact, as I tell clients, if we don't need a lover, then why are they even in our lives in the first place? While there are billions of people in this world, there are not billions of people that we could connect with—where we'd feel that reaction of two souls colliding who have known each other before.

People are not interchangeable. So when we've met someone we feel like we need in our lives for whatever reason, it's okay.

NO LOVE IS BETTER THAN ANOTHER

Everything is a cycle, and everything is related to a previous lesson.

We can't understand forever love until we've been hurt, until we admit we need someone, until we grasp our own personal value, and until we learn that we can't fit just anyone into the role of spouse or boyfriend and have it be as fulfilling or meaningful. The one misconception that often occurs in our love lives is that we deem one love "better" than another; we say that our soul mate love was good, but that our twin flame love is the best. We think the love that lasts forever is somehow better than the one that only lasted a few months.

The truth is that there is no one love that is better than another, because love cannot be quantified in such a way.

We say "I love you so much," but *much* implies an amount and there is no way to measure the amount of love that we feel. We say one love is better than another because it's a simpler way of saying that we're feeling more fulfilled, happier, more successful, at peace, or even having more amazing sex; but none of that means one love was better than another and it certainly doesn't mean one lover was better than another.

Twin flames are supposed to teach each other about themselves. We are supposed to wake each other up to be a better version of ourselves, to be more aware, conscious, and honest about our desires and wants. So, when we sometimes say this feels like the best love, what we're really saying is this is the love in which we feel like our best selves. This is the love that feels like it fits the best, even if it's not something we ever considered before.

This is the love that inspires me, that challenges me to grow and be honest with myself. It's this love that doesn't let me get by with doing the same old crap I've always done; it makes me want to do better, be better—and so we then start to believe that this love is better when really it's the love that helps us be better for ourselves.

When we start to feel like we're becoming our best selves, it feels like we're waking up from a fog and from being stuck in patterns that have felt limiting. We start to see more clearly, not just love, not just the world, but—most important—ourselves. Waking up to our best possible selves is like suddenly seeing that we used the baggage from other people to keep us in place and hold us down.

We built walls around who we thought we were or what we deserved, what we were capable of, and even how we loved, simply because we were only seeing ourselves through the lens of others.

Twins are so special because we are finally able to truly see ourselves, our amazingness and also those areas where we still need to grow. We're not using the eyes of our parents, our friends, or society but finally just seeing our essence: the person we were born to be before we started to absorb the doubts and beliefs of others.

Sofia had been through all her loves and was living with Felipe, her twin flame, when she and I connected. She had been exploring some ideas about what it really meant to journey through these loves and wanted some greater clarification so she would know in what direction to take the relationship with Felipe.

When we first started our sessions, she described her first love, her soul mate, as a nice guy but ultimately the relationship was pretty bad; and her second—her karmic love—as being awful. I asked her to describe what made her use those negative adjectives for those relationships. She said it was because the experiences themselves weren't pleasant. But I asked her, "Does that really mean Felipe is any 'better'? Or only healthier, more aligned?"

As she paused, I explained to her that everything in nature, in the divine world, is a balance of both positive and negative but depending on how we want to view it, we then call it bad or good. I even asked, "Was everything with your soul mate or karmic love bad? Did you have no good times or memories come from them?" "Of course not," she replied.

So I pointed out that this relationship with Felipe isn't necessarily any better—but rather she'd changed how she experienced love.

In the end, we understand that there is no love better than another, that each had to happen regardless, whether it was only three loves or if there is a list of names so long, we can barely remember them all. We come to learn that we are who we are in *this* moment because of all of our various lives that we have experienced. Yet it's our twin flame, our forever love, who inspires us to become our best self, who helps us heal, and also shows us what love truly is.

It's the connection that tears down any of those lingering walls or false ideologies in order for us to get back to that essence; and so we come to realize during this phase that it's not just that we need them—but that we need them in order to become and be our best self.

FOREVER LOVE ISN'T HAPPILY EVER AFTER

We don't need to marry our twin flame.

We might not even necessarily need to have any sort of conventional relationship with them. But we do need them not only in order to be our best selves, but to continue to grow into whatever that might mean tomorrow so that we can actually live these best lives we see hashtagged all around us. We need our twin flame to hold us accountable, to trigger us, to not let us take the easy way out or make excuses for us.

Whether we call them a twin flame or not doesn't actually change the fact that it's only our third love who will encourage us to forever love ourselves.

In the 2016 movie *La La Land*, actor Ryan Gosling plays Sebastian, an aspiring jazz musician, opposite Mia, a struggling actress played by Emma Stone. In this slow-to-start romance, these two keep getting thrown together. Yet even once they have fallen in love, they realize that doesn't guarantee anything.

Even though they originally came together because of their shared dreams and ambitions, they soon realize that they need more than just each other to make their love a reality. That life will continue to throw obstacles at them and that just as they chose their careers, they will have to keep choosing each other in order to actually have their love last forever. But to choose another means to first know ourselves and understand that there will never be a perfect love. There will be one, however, that never quits. As Gosling's character Sebastian says, "It's conflict and it's compromise and it's just . . . It's new every time." In many ways, that perfectly sums up the twin flame connection and this journey toward a forever love.

Because we will have conflict, both with our lover and with ourselves, we will have to compromise—but there's also that newness, that feeling of inexhaustible love. That feeling that lets us believe in love again.

That magic.

See, this forever love is so much more than just a happily-ever-after. It's also about realizing, learning, and rooting ourselves in such a deep love for ourselves that we have no choice but to choose the love that loves us in a similar way. This love for ourselves began possibly a million years ago when we first had our hearts broken by our soul mate; it began when we had to start seeing that life might go differently than we had anticipated and that perhaps we didn't have things figured out after all.

Developing self-love is a journey, just like learning the ins and outs of unconditional love for another. Yet in order to offer it to a partner, to our twin flame—we first have to give it to ourselves.

Now sometimes people call bullshit on this; they don't believe that we have to love ourselves in order to be loved (insert eyeroll). There is a difference, though, in just being loved and in being loved in a healthy way. There's a difference between the love of a fleeting romance and the one who can know how you are feeling by taking one look into your eyes. And there's a big difference between the love that demands you do something for it and the love that shows up before you even asked.

So, no, you don't need to love yourself before being loved—but you do before you find that third love. Otherwise, for lack of a better explanation, you'll just keep dating assholes and having your heart broken.

The real secret to finding our twin flame is learning how to unconditionally love ourselves.

This journey is one that sometimes takes a few years or perhaps an entire lifetime. It's the unraveling of self, the unlearning of all the bullshit we were told to be and expect, it's letting go of body image language that grows within our minds from the time we're little girls—or boys. To learn how to truly love ourselves is to understand that the love from another will never determine our worth or value. It's to understand that while we may need someone, it's not that someone who defines us. It's not that person's job to fill in our blanks or to be a mask for our insecurities. It's not even their job to love us fiercely enough to make our lack of self-love disappear.

As we go through this journey, we realize that we were never in search of the best love or even the best relationship—we were actually in pursuit of our best selves.

It wasn't that any ex didn't love us enough but rather we didn't love ourselves enough. We didn't love ourselves enough to walk away when all the signs of destruction were there, we didn't love ourselves enough to steer clear of Mr. Emotionally Unavailable, and we didn't love ourselves enough to hold out for what we knew we deserved. So we chose lessons, we chose pain and chaos. Even in the testing phase of our third love, we may need to learn to unconditionally love ourselves.

To not need validation from another, to be confident in ourselves and our pursuits, to be able to be our own advocate and to understand that no matter what, no matter who may come or who may leave—we are still loved when we truly have that love for self.

But we had to go through everything that we did to reach this point, and if while reading this you realize that you're still in progress—that's great. It's great because you're on this journey, you haven't taken the easy way out by having someone next to you tonight only to have a warm body, someone who doesn't really foster that growth. It's great that you're becoming aware that there is no love that's better than another—but only one that helps you become a better version of yourself.

Perhaps it's simplistic to say that we choose partners based on how we feel about ourselves. But we also choose lovers because of how we *want* to feel about ourselves, a big difference. For many of us, early in our romantic journey, we chose our soul mate and karmic passion because they perpetuated our wounds and fed our addiction. They extended the conditioning we grew up with and they reflected where we were mentally and emotionally at that time.

As we went through these experiences, however, we changed, we grew—or are in the processing of growing now—and we no longer need to date men who ghost us simply because our father left when we were young. We don't need to date women who mirror our mother and her lack of confidence in us, and we don't need to take home that bartender (even if he is cute) just because we're afraid of dying alone with our cats.

Jane, an incredibly creative and thoughtful woman, reached out because she was confused about her twin flame relationship. As we spoke the first time, it came out that she had met her twin a couple years ago, they both were aware they were twin flames, but they weren't in the place yet to be together.

They had an un-relationship: together but not physically, because of their own journeys and because they lived in separate countries. They both had committed to not being sexually intimate with anyone else as long as that felt right for them; they spoke often, and saw each other every few months.

But then Jane began to feel restless and she became interested in one of the men she surfed with on a regular basis. She called me because she felt like she was on the brink. Should she stay committed to her twin flame or explore things with the cute surfer? Together we spoke about patterns and cycles. She said that two years earlier, she just would have taken him home and never even thought about it, so in itself this conversation was already part of a different cycle.

After speaking with me several times, Jane admitted that she was tired of the long distance and wanted a greater commitment from her twin flame because she did care for him. So instead of just going to bed with the cute surfer—she talked to her twin and they made a plan.

In this way, she broke her cycle of leaving when it got hard because the connection with her twin flame was worth her stepping up to do her own self-work.

This is how twin flames help each other grow in ways different from any other relationship.

Once we've been involved with our twin flame and begin to feel ourselves waking up to that unconditional love, only then will we be able to choose a partner who reflects that back to us. While it's similar to the lessons of worthiness and deserving that we had to learn up to this point, this building block of self-love is the last piece because we will only ever be able to accept the love from another that we've already given to ourselves.

We will only be able to accept unconditional love from our twin flame once we have given it to ourselves, once we have learned who we are apart from any partner, apart from any fear, insecurity, or loneliness—only once we have faced our demons and risen even stronger because of them. When we get to this place, however, needing our twin flame, recognizing the value that they—and likewise we—bring to our lives creates an entirely different dynamic.

It's learning that while no one love was ever better than another, not just anyone could help us grow into our best selves, and that when we say that a particular love is the best, what we're really saying is that it's the love that allows us to feel like we can be our best selves. We choose the people, the partnerships, and the relationships that either contribute to us perpetuating our wounding or help us heal into our best selves. We choose people to continue a cycle or to begin a new one.

No one comes into this life knowing how to love themselves or knowing what it means to choose a healthy relationship; and while maybe that's not of highest importance to everyone, it is becoming something that more and more people are not just aware of but actually desiring to build.

CONSCIOUS CHOICES

We still have to choose our twin flame.

The interesting dynamic about twins is that while we didn't and couldn't choose a particular person to be our third love, it's still a love that we have to choose to accept, because this is a journey of self. We only come together because we are committed to our own personal work; and so while we may love our twin, we may be in that constant-contact pseudo-relationship status—we can't actually choose them until we have chosen ourselves.

When we know what we need, desire, want, even what our non-negotiables are, and when we can love ourselves through, around, and in and out of all of it—then, and only then, will we be able to not only see the value in our twin, but also be able to choose to accept them as well. While there is so much magic, divine timing, and chemistry that's associated with this love—it's also very real. It's so real, in fact, that we need to get real with ourselves before we can even look at our twin flame.

It's the love that will continually challenge us but will love us wildly at the same time.

One important part of this type of challenge is the supportive growth that occurs. Again, while this mainly arises in the early stages of this journey, it's actually something that will continue forever, perhaps not to the degree that occurs in the beginning, but it's that accountability factor of always having someone there who won't tell you what you want to hear—but what you need to hear.

We can't grow in the same ways without our twin flame because we will remain blind to those areas we need to focus on the most. In life, we're able to see only our physical selves; in twin flame relationships, we see our emotional selves, the mental wounds that only we can heal for ourselves—not because we don't need another person, but because no one can do our work for us.

We can't grow without being challenged, without that pushback. Our twin flame mirrors our default behaviors, our conditioning, all of our self-limiting thoughts—essentially all the areas we need to push through, to learn from, not only in order to truly grow, but to become our best selves. Blocks keep us from unconditionally loving ourselves, which then prevents us from accepting love from another. A twin flame will love you unconditionally, but will also say, "Hey, this is all your shit. I'm not gonna sugarcoat it and I'm not gonna let you escape it because I love you. And that means helping you to become your best self even if the growth has to come before the love or relationship."

This means that we sometimes may need to love our twin flame from a distance while we do our own work and they do theirs, as was the case with Jane and her twin. It may mean that we have to temporarily let them go or even just surrender to the journey and trust the process. This may even mean that in those moments they might not be ready to choose us because they're still learning how to choose themselves.

The love that is shared is not conditional on any of that.

It's not just about shoveling the snow from the driveway, bringing us chocolates, or even kissing our warm bare skin beneath the moon. This kind of love reaches beyond the physical to the spiritual. This third love doesn't say *"I love you if"* but rather *"I love you regardless."*

Yet to be able to love in such a way, we also have to have an extraordinary trust and faith not just in the connection, but in ourselves. During my own journey with my twin flame, there was a time when I first began to realize I was at this place and in truth was petrified and in pain myself because I didn't want to walk away from him or love. I didn't want to leave him; and more than anything, I wanted to be there for him just as I had always been. But sometimes we have a feeling, a knowing that we're meant to be apart for a while—not because we're giving up on the other person, but because we know in our hearts that they can only do the work they need to if they aren't with us and we can only do ours alone as well.

This is very different from the running or testing phase. This usually occurs after being in significant connection for some time and knowing that, as much as we have grown with and because of our twin, this part must be done alone. There was a time, crying over the phone, I sobbed to my lover that I wished I could help him with what he was going through, but that I just didn't think I was meant to. It scared me, because I loved him and wanted to help. But I stayed away anyway. In that moment, the greatest way for me to show him I loved him was to let him go. To let him experience life on his own and to grow in his strength and awareness for himself. It wasn't because the love wasn't forever, but because sometimes the hardest test of love is letting go and trusting that if or when we are meant to come back together—we will.

There have been clients I've worked with who have disregarded their twin flame as only another karmic love, not because this person truly was, but because they were searching for answers and attempted to classify the relationship so that it could be dismissed because of its difficulty.

When I met Tanya, she had been involved with her twin flame for five years. During this time, their relationship was increasingly passionate and was generally very easy—even though they each had their own challenges to overcome. She not only wanted this to be her forever, but she truly felt she had reached her final destination on her journey to love.

But then Nick began acting differently. He started to express uncertainty about what he was bringing to the relationship and also worried he no longer knew who he was or what he was passionate about. During this rocky time, he began pursuing things with an ex and cut things off with Tanya, telling her, "I am my best self with Julie, not you. I'll be your friend, but I can't be anything more."

Tanya was devastated, yet—while she loved him—she knew she couldn't be his friend because she'd never be able to move on. This was a man with whom she felt a connection that defied what she had thought was possible. She truly accepted him for who he was: loving him unconditionally no matter what they had been through.

During our conversations after this occurred, she wanted to just disregard him as a karmic love. She told me that she felt as if, in the end, he was just another repetition of the cycle because she hadn't

learned what she was meant to. She tried to label him and their relationship any way she could to find closure. She became certain
that one label, "wound mate," truly described their bond. A wound
mate is similar to a karmic love in that the relationship reveals the
healing that still needs to be done; but a wound mate is often found
so that we can escape our own growth indefinitely and ultimately
remain wounded.

While the wound in question can be different for each of us, it
likely will be tied into feelings about abandonment, self-worth, and
emotional availability. We stay with a wound mate because unconsciously we enjoy the pain of being wounded—it's familiar and to
leave our wound mate would mean we'd have to let go of that aspect
of ourselves that identifies with being the victim.

But still Tanya couldn't ascribe this label or any other to her relationship with Nick. She couldn't classify him as just a karmic love
because of their deep spiritual connection, and she couldn't disregard him as a narcissist, since he had such an incredible heart.

So, she tried to move on, not understanding the purpose of what
had happened and not being able to make sense of it. She spent time
healing and then decided to get back out there—but nothing stuck.
No other man decided to show up to pursue things with her more
than just casually dating, and she was not physically intimate with
anyone else.

A year after they broke up, Nick returned.

While he returned with apologies, he also offered an explanation
and a plan—not just for his future, but for the one he still hoped was
a possibility with Tanya. Nick told her that he could now see he

ran back to the security of his ex because, even though it wasn't everything he needed, it was still comfortable. In their time apart, he learned that he still had work to do on himself: on his confidence and in healing some of his wounds around love and feelings of being worthy.

They took things slowly this time, approached things differently, and spoke more honestly about their needs. And while neither of them would want to repeat the time they spent apart, they do believe it served a purpose for greater healing for them both.

Time is the truest barometer of what type of connection you have, because even twin flames don't make the right choice all the time. Sometimes our forever love needs to take a detour. In these situations, though, it's not about self-sacrificing or trying to fix the other person. It's not about simply taking what we are offered, but in holding steady to our boundaries and knowing what we deserve.

It's about acceptance for our reality in that moment.

We can't mess things up with our twin flame. We can't lose someone who is meant to be our forever, so in those moments when it feels like our world has shifted completely and nothing makes sense, the only thing we can do is keep living. Trust in the universe and believe that even if we don't understand it in this moment, everything does happen for a reason—including times of separation. We can definitely grow within other connections, but there's an intensity and a depth that is present in our twin flame that can't be fulfilled by just anyone.

This is not a one-size-fits-all kind of love.

And so we learn to not just surrender to this love, but we learn to receive it—to accept it, not because we need it to supplement parts we're lacking, but because we learned that there was never any lack to begin with. The only barriers were the ones that we had set up ourselves.

THE ONE

Sometimes we find that we're the one we've been searching for.

It is this love that shows us that we were never searching for The One but rather were on the journey to become the one for ourselves, so we could eventually show up in that way for another—not because we are superhumans who have no need for anyone, but because being our best selves means understanding that we're still a work in progress. It's understanding that if we don't offer ourselves love and forgiveness, then we will never be able to accept it from a partner.

And so perhaps none of this is about finding our forever love, but in reality, learning how to accept it. Love finds us. Our twin flame finds us, usually when we wish they wouldn't. Magic finds us, but so does reality. The good times find us, but so do the bad. And the doubts. But in the end—so does faith.

The lesson with our third love is to understand that the love we possess, the love we feel, isn't only because we have our twin flame with us laughing as we take a road trip under the stars or because we're pressed up against each other in the shower, but rather they were the ones to help wake us up to discovering the deep well of self-love that we now have for ourselves or are in the process of learning.

We care for our third love in the way that we do because they are the one to not only help us become our best selves but also to teach us how to love ourselves.

Not because they were necessarily the best, but because we became our best with them.

The reason that this relationship not only feels as intense as it does but also lasts is because the twin flame is the only relationship that helps us see that we were never lacking anything. We were never *not* whole, we were never wrong for sensing we were meant for a different life, or for believing in a love that's far richer than any silver-screen romance.

Yes, our twin flame feels like The One—but so do we.

This means that in many ways, once each twin has developed that self-love for themselves and opened up to receive it from their partner, a whole new journey begins—learning how to actually be an *us*.

Despite the ups and downs, the challenges, and the tests, it's the underlying feeling of unconditional love that has always connected us with our third love. It's not because of a piece of paper, an obligation to do the right thing, or anything else that kept us coming back (or that made us finally realize there was no leaving)—it was always only love.

This is just the beginning of a lifelong adventure of growing and learning, but most of all, loving.

You Never Know When You'll
Stumble into Love

We all desire to not just fall in love—but to be part of that "once in a lifetime" love story.

None of us wants to be seen as average, or to think that we have just a regular relationship. We all want to be different. We desire to know that we have something that is unique to only us, because then we feel more protective of or connected to it.

If we all believed that love was merely convenient, and any person would do, marriage or a relationship would be nothing more than a contract we sign on the dotted line. And perhaps for some, that is the path that they are meant to take in this lifetime. But even then I have to wonder, why?

Why wouldn't we want to believe that we all end up with the one person in this entire world that we were created with? What's so scary or impossible about believing that there is one person in this world who fits us more than anyone else?

It seems that as a society we are born into the blindness of skepticism. It doesn't matter if as little girls we wore veils and said "I do" as we married our best friends in pretend games of wedding, or that as we grew we were told we were foolish for thinking that love could be such a thing.

But that's where we have to stop.

Because who ever told you love shouldn't be fucking amazing?

And why on earth did you start believing them?

I understand that it has taken you a lifetime already to get here. Perhaps you are reading these words with tears watering your beautiful eyes because you wondered if you could actually ever get the one thing you always said you believed in—love.

But, seriously, let me correct that: you don't just want love. You want all of it. You want the warrior who is passionate, gentle, sensitive, loyal, and funny, and who will see you in the morning looking like a hot mess and not run for the hills. You want adventure, and moments under the midnight moon across the oceans of the world.

You want to feel understood.

Perhaps more than anything, though, you just don't ever want to think that you made a mistake in love.

We all like to be right, but there is a point at which needing to be right, when it comes to love, is as detrimental as slipping a noose over our neck and hoping to still be able to breathe. You can be right, or you can be in love. It's as simple as that. What we have wanted from love in the past is changing, and not only is that okay, it's amazing, because we're searching out someone who is a soul partner—not just a life partner.

We don't want meat loaf on Wednesdays and sex on Friday night—we want a life of awe-inspiring possibility where at the end of it all our love has stood for something greater than just a way to reproduce or fit into a mold that someone else has cast. No longer are we satisfied by those unions that are convenient or that seem to fulfill specific ideals that our families or society have taught us we should aspire to.

And that's amazing, because we should be inspired to find our own kind of love.

So we love. And we love again. And even again. We love until we find our twin flame.

We give chances, and we learn along the way. We give the best parts of ourselves up to that desire for something more, and along the way we come to understand that there is no fairy-tale love. There is no perfect person and no perfect relationship, but only that unto-itself love, which will always be perfect.

On this journey, we stop thinking that there are right ones and wrong ones. We stop comparing loves and understand that one is not any better than the other. We start to see that who we are in the moment when we meet someone will reflect more on the relationship than the actual person themselves. We understand that we will gravitate toward those who are meant to teach us lessons and we will manifest what we fear or desire depending on what we are radiating.

But in the end of everything, love is just love.

It's the feeling that, while indescribable, is the deep admiration for another. Through the challenges that we face and the joys that we experience, we start to see that in order to attract that forever love, we first need to fall in love with ourselves. So we become aware of patterns, of cycles. We start to make different choices, which is just the beginning of receiving what it is that we hope to receive.

Because while no love is better than another, there will be one person who, like a key fitting into a lock, will be able to open us up in ways that no one ever has before, or ever will again. We will understand that it's impossible to ever love in the same way twice, and so how we understand and practice love will have to change as well.

We will never love another as we did our sweet soul mate, and we will never love in the same addictive cycles that we did our karmic. We might have three soul mates or maybe only one. We might have ten karmic partners before we finally learn our lessons, or maybe just two. But there will be one. One person. One love that regardless of the label or title we give it, regardless of whether we marry, will be the person who forever changes us and how we love.

One person who will be our twin flame and who will forever change the relationship we have with ourselves.

There will be one person who will love us in all the ways we've always desired—in the very same ways that we needed to learn to do for ourselves. The very same person who will rip down our walls and make us question everything, the person who will open our eyes to a world we never knew existed.

We can call this person our twin flame, but in truth they are just themselves: an ordinary person who learned how to love extraordinarily. They are unique, they are whole, they are above any sort of definition not because of superpowers but because they stayed when they could have gone, they made it work when they could have given up, and they loved when by all accounts it seemed impossible.

They helped us become more of ourselves, more of who we were meant to be. The one that was always there, but perhaps we didn't know how to get hold of. The person who was meant to awaken us to what possibilities lingered outside of the realm of what's real, and the one who showed us that to love ourselves wasn't to do anything but accept ourselves as we already are—just as they do.

It's the journey to finding our forever love, which always has and always will remain with us. Learning that we have to be who we truly are, we have to make the choice to commit to ourselves and to our own truth before we can live in union with another. But it's also to understand and accept that within this process, our humanity will show. We will hurt the person we say we love, we will make mistakes, and we will try again because it's love.

And love is always worth it. Worth anything.

This is not just the journey to love, but also to learning what love isn't. It's to no longer need to participate in relationships with those who are emotionally unavailable or are just playing games. It's to know we're worth more than booty calls, and that if we actually want to attract what we want, then we have to start making choices that align with it.

But it's also about never giving up. Never sacrificing and never letting our ego or pride get in the way of doing what matters most—loving.

Love stories are not linear, and perhaps we may find out as time goes by that the person we thought was our karmic partner was a soul mate, maybe our soul mate will seem like our twin flame, and maybe our twin flame will resemble a karmic love at times. We may get turned around trying to figure out what someone is, or what their purpose is in our lives, instead of just loving them, just seeing where the journey will take us, rather than thinking the journey is meant to end with a breakup or whispering "I do" under starry skies.

It's learning that no one knows what we need but ourselves, and that what matters most isn't what we call love but what that love represents to us. It's accepting that not knowing is a part of the journey, and that while we can hope we have it all figured out, life has a way of showing us that we were all wrong. But it's also being okay that we were wrong, it's trusting that not only will we learn what we're meant to, we'll know what we need to when we're meant to—and above all, we will always end up exactly where we're meant to.

And with whom.

Love is magic. It's indescribable, it's moonlit nights and kisses that seem to get lost along the edge of time; but it's also hard days and tearstained faces. It's not knowing where to go from here but trusting we're on the right path. It's forgiveness. And forgiveness again. Forgiveness for ourselves. For our partner, and for just plain not being able to do better despite how hard we wish we could or tried to do.

It's not giving up but also not persisting with lost causes. It's truth, trust, and above all faith that this person we've shown parts of ourselves to will try their best to not betray us—and then it's forgiveness again when they do.

Finding our forever love is learning to be comfortable in our singleness, it's dating ourselves and having weekends away with our girlfriends in which we flirt with cute guys and drink more martinis than water. It's going to bed alone because we'd rather wake up with no regrets.

It's about learning it's not our job to please our parents. It's not our responsibility to fit into society or somehow follow a blueprint for our lives. It's being okay to be different. To want something it sometimes seems no one else craves. It's understanding our strengths and admitting when we're wrong, because we ended up somewhere so much better than we could have predicted. And above all, it's about being able to wake up each morning and be willing to try again.

Love is about not closing down, even when it hurts. It's not self-protecting or sabotaging just to keep people away, and it's not keeping your heart in a cage because you're scared of being hurt again. It's about opening up your heart instead of thinking that love will never come again. The journey to finding our forever love is to understand that pain is part of the process. We have to get broken open so we can let more love in. Relationships have to fail so we can learn what not to do next time. And sometimes we have to let the one who got away in fact leave, so that we can realize we don't want to live without them.

This is about us giving up the bullshit of having to be hard. Of not catching feelings or coming off as too emotional. It's about giving up everything that the world tells us we have to be or do in order to attract a partner, and realizing that the one who will love you forever won't actually care if your roots are touched up or if you have a pimple the size of Texas on your chin. It's seeing that we're messy, life is messy, and love is definitely messy but that we will commit to it.

We commit to trying because no matter how many times love knocks us down, there will be a time when it stretches out its hand to help us up.

When we're walking alone in a new city and bump into someone coming out of a cab only to have our world turned upside down. Or when we give in to the dreams we've been having of our ex and reach out only to find they've been dreaming of us too. It will come when it's meant to. It will come again. For the first time, or even return for the umpteenth try.

But it will come again.

Because this entire search for love isn't a science; its purpose is not to quantify it, but to learn from it. To remain open to it. To have faith in it. In yourself and in this journey. It's to make a commitment to not lose yourself in a relationship, but to not hold back either. It's to understand that we can't take anything personally and just because someone says no doesn't mean they are saying no to us. It's to revel so deep within the love we hold for ourselves that we realize we're never without it.

We never lack love even when we're single because of how deeply we love ourselves.

And so, we start to make different choices. We stop rushing. Planning. Thinking we know everything or even wanting to pretend that we do. We give up our fallbacks and we stop swiping dating apps late at night knowing that it's not someone to go to bed with that we want—but someone to wake up to.

It's accepting that we want it all but only because we have given all to ourselves first. We've learned to not hold back love or acceptance from ourselves. We've learned we're worthy of amazing things simply because we already are. We accept that we want independence *and* companionship. We want alone time *and* someone to go to bed with each evening. We want to run wild and free across this great big beautiful world, *and* we want someone at home cheering us on.

This journey is about learning not just who we are or what love is, but how we need to be loved to become our best selves; to continue to grow into that version of ourselves that we won't ever give up on. And so we actually get to the point of prioritizing love and relationships. We stop searching for love. We stop trying to make it happen. We stop trying to wake someone up to what we are or what we share. We stop believing that we have control over everything, and we start simply being. Existing in love because we are love. We love ourselves and we love the possibility of what's to come even though we have no idea what that will be.

And we become okay with that. We come to be at peace with it.

That's the moment that changes everything.

That's the moment we stumble into love again, and we realize that it is never something that can be forced, or talked into—never even something we were ever without. Instead, it's something we were on a journey toward this entire time.

A journey of letting our twin flame find us—and being ready for it when they do.

ACKNOWLEDGMENTS

I can't speak about my journey of writing without mentioning Elephant Journal. Thank you for being the first platform to publish my words, and to Ashleigh Jai Hitchcock for being my first editor and teaching me how to be a better writer. I am forever grateful to author Matthew Kelly for reaching out after reading my words on Elephant Journal and being the one to motivate me to write my first book. His encouragement and help along the way, including connecting me to my fantastic agent, Joseph Durepos, forever changed my life and made this book possible—thank you. To Sara Carder, Rachel Ayotte, and all those at TarcherPerigee, thank you for believing in me; for seeing the possibility within this book, and for all your support, work, and guidance to make this a reality. Lastly, to my family: to my daughters for being content with cereal for dinner when Momma was writing all day; and to my parents, without whose help in caring for my girls while I worked long days this book might not have ever been written. I am eternally grateful for all of you. Thank you. xx

KATE ROSE received her B.A. in Visual Arts Education from Mount Mary University and an M.S. in Clinical Art Therapy from Springfield College, while volunteering in the AmeriCorps Program as a leader of youth programming in an inner-city environment. She worked as an art therapist with children who have severe social and emotional disorders for more than ten years before beginning her writing and adult counseling career.

Kate has published more than one thousand articles on the topics of love, relationships, family, parenting, divorce, sex, astrology, and twin flames across numerous platforms, including Elephant Journal and YourTango. She has also built a private international coaching practice specializing in self-love and relationships and also leads yearly women's empowerment retreats across the globe. Kate lives in the Hidden Hills of Massachusetts with her daughters, twelve-year-old Emma and seven-year-old Abigail, and their three cats. Sometimes, you can find them dancing in the rain and having tea parties at sunset, but mostly they're just making as many memories as they can and living life to the fullest each day.